GOVERNMENT PROCEDURES AND OPERATIONS

FEDERAL GRANT MANAGEMENT AND CONTROLS

SELECT ASSESSMENTS

GOVERNMENT PROCEDURES AND OPERATIONS

Additional books in this series can be found on Nova's website under the Series tab.

Additional e-books in this series can be found on Nova's website under the e-book tab.

GOVERNMENT PROCEDURES AND OPERATIONS

FEDERAL GRANT MANAGEMENT AND CONTROLS

SELECT ASSESSMENTS

DANA T. GREER
EDITOR

nova publishers
New York

Library of Congress Cataloging-in-Publication Data

ISBN: 978-1-63482-559-7

Published by Nova Science Publishers, Inc. † New York

Contents

PREFACE

This book examines whether the five largest grant-making agencies' internal control oversight processes for their grant programs were consistent with OMB requirements and describes internal control issues that have been reported related to the grants management process and key grant programs. The book also examines federal, state, and local experiences with implementing grants funded by the Recovery Act by identifying examples of good practices employed and challenges faced in meeting the act's accountability and transparency requirements. Finally, the book examines the extent to which selected federal agencies and grantees have mechanisms and guidance in place to distinguish between administrative and program costs and to facilitate the availability of these data to Congress and the public; and the extent to which there are challenges that hinder the comparability of grant administrative cost data.

Chapter 1 – In fiscal year 2013, the federal government obligated over $555 billion for grants. Effective oversight of internal controls is important for providing reasonable assurance that grants are awarded properly, recipients are eligible, and federal grant funds are used as intended.

GAO was asked to review internal control issues over grants. This report (1) examines whether the five largest grant-making agencies' internal control oversight processes for their grant programs were consistent with OMB requirements and (2) describes internal control issues that have been reported related to the grants management process and key grant programs.

To achieve these objectives, GAO reviewed the fiscal year 2012 internal control assessment processes for the five largest grant-making agencies' grants programs, as conducted under OMB Circular No. A-123. GAO reviewed the agencies' assessment documentation and reviewed grants internal control findings reported in other reviews of these agencies for fiscal years 2012 and

2013. GAO did not include Medicaid—the largest federal grant program—which has been well covered in other GAO and HHS OIG reviews.

GAO is not making any recommendations but continues to monitor grants management as part of its work on key issues.

In general, the five agencies concurred with the information in the report. Some agencies also provided technical comments that were incorporated, as appropriate.

Chapter 2 – The federal government spends billions of dollars on various grants to achieve diverse purposes. The total cost of a grant includes both program costs that directly support the grant's mission and services and administrative costs to run the program. These administrative activities, such as managing finances, are essential. It is important for agencies to track the cost of these activities to provide accountability for efficient use of federal resources.

GAO was asked to review how costs associated with the administration of grants are tracked and the availability of this information. GAO examined (1) the extent to which selected federal agencies and grantees have mechanisms and guidance in place to distinguish between administrative and program costs and to facilitate the availability of these data to Congress and the public; and (2) the extent to which there are challenges that hinder the comparability of grant administrative cost data. For this review GAO selected six grant programs—three in HHS and three in the Department of Housing and Urban Development (HUD). Agencies and grant programs were selected in part based on obligation amounts and grant types. GAO reviewed each program's statutes, regulations, guidance, and grant documents, as applicable, and interviewed agency officials. Although GAO's findings are not generalizable, they are indicative of the wide variation associated with the mechanisms and guidance for tracking grant administrative costs.

GAO received and incorporated, as appropriate, technical comments from HHS. HUD did not provide comments.

Chapter 3 – In response to the recent serious recession, Congress enacted the Recovery Act to promote economic recovery, make investments, and minimize or avoid reductions in state and local government services. Approximately $219 billion was distributed as grants for use in states and localities, making grants a major component of the act. These grants covered a broad range of areas including education, transportation, energy, infrastructure, the environment, health care, and housing.

GAO was asked to examine grant management lessons learned resulting from the Recovery Act. This report examines federal, state, and local experiences with implementing grants funded by the Recovery Act by identifying examples of good practices employed and challenges faced in meeting the act's accountability and transparency requirements. GAO reviewed relevant documents including OMB and Recovery Board guidance, relevant literature, and previous reports by GAO, federal inspectors general, and others. GAO also interviewed officials from OMB, the Recovery Board, four federal agencies, three state governments, and two local governments, among others. This report also draws on GAO's past bimonthly reviews of selected states' and localities' use of Recovery funds.

In: Federal Grant Management and Controls ISBN: 978-1-63482-559-7
Editor: Dana T. Greer

Chapter 1

FEDERAL GRANTS: AGENCIES PERFORMED INTERNAL CONTROL ASSESSMENTS CONSISTENT WITH GUIDANCE AND ARE ADDRESSING INTERNAL CONTROL DEFICIENCIES*

United States Government Accountability Office

ABBREVIATIONS

ACF	Administration for Children and Families
CFDA	Catalog of Federal Domestic Assistance
CHIP	Children's Health Insurance Program
CMS	Centers for Medicare & Medicaid Services
CPD	Office of Community and Planning Development
DOT	Department of Transportation
FFMIA	Federal Financial Management Improvement Act of 1996
FHWA	Federal Highway Administration
FMFIA	Federal Managers' Financial Integrity Act of 1982
FNS	Food and Nutrition Service
FSA	Federal Student Aid

* This is an edited, reformatted and augmented version of The United States Government Accountability Office publication, GAO-14-539, dated July 2014.

FTA	Federal Transit Administration
HHS	Department of Health and Human Services
HUD	Department of Urban Development
IPERA	Improper Payments Elimination and Recovery Act of 2010
IPIA	Improper Payments Information Act of 2002
NIFA	National Institute of Food and Agriculture
NIH	National Institutes of Health
OESE	Office of Elementary and Secondary Education
OIG	Office of Inspector General
OMB	Office of Management and Budget
OSERS	Office of Special Education and Rehabilitative Services
PIH	Office of Public and Indian Housing
USDA	Department of Agriculture

WHY GAO DID THIS STUDY

In fiscal year 2013, the federal government obligated over $555 billion for grants. Effective oversight of internal controls is important for providing reasonable assurance that grants are awarded properly, recipients are eligible, and federal grant funds are used as intended.

GAO was asked to review internal control issues over grants. This report (1) examines whether the five largest grant-making agencies' internal control oversight processes for their grant programs were consistent with OMB requirements and (2) describes internal control issues that have been reported related to the grants management process and key grant programs.

To achieve these objectives, GAO reviewed the fiscal year 2012 internal control assessment processes for the five largest grant-making agencies' grants programs, as conducted under OMB Circular No. A-123. GAO reviewed the agencies' assessment documentation and reviewed grants internal control findings reported in other reviews of these agencies for fiscal years 2012 and 2013. GAO did not include Medicaid—the largest federal grant program—which has been well covered in other GAO and HHS OIG reviews.

GAO is not making any recommendations but continues to monitor grants management as part of its work on key issues.

In general, the five agencies concurred with the information in the report. Some agencies also provided technical comments that were incorporated, as appropriate.

WHAT GAO FOUND

For fiscal year 2012, the processes used by the five largest grant-making agencies to conduct their internal control assessments were consistent with the requirements of Office of Management and Budget (OMB) Circular No. A-123, which requires that agencies identify significant areas within their operations in which to implement key controls, continuously monitor and test those controls, and report annually on management's judgment regarding the adequacy and effectiveness of internal control. The five largest grant-making agencies by amount of grant obligations are the Departments of Health and Human Services (HHS), Education, Transportation (DOT), Agriculture (USDA), and Housing and Urban Development (HUD). The agencies identified areas of risk, including grants programs and grants management processes, in which to implement key controls and then monitored and tested those controls. The agencies identified deficiencies through control tests, prepared and implemented corrective action plans to address the deficiencies identified, and reported on their internal control through annual management assurance statements. HHS, DOT, and USDA qualified their internal control management assurance statements for fiscal year 2012, in part because of material weaknesses affecting their grant programs. For fiscal year 2013, HHS, USDA, and HUD gave qualified statements of assurance in part because of material weaknesses in their grant programs.

In addition to issues identified through the OMB Circular No. A-123 process, other audits and reviews have reported internal control issues related to the grants management process and grant programs. For example:

- For fiscal years 2012 and 2013, DOT's financial statement auditors reported that DOT did not timely identify and deobligate unused grant obligations. DOT took actions to address the recommendations, resulting in the auditors reducing the issue from a material weakness in fiscal year 2012 to a significant deficiency in fiscal year 2013.
- In July 2013, HUD's Office of Inspector General (OIG) reported that guidance for ensuring whether grantees are carrying out grant activities in a timely manner in compliance with requirements of the Community Development Block Grant program was not always implemented effectively. HUD generally concurred with the recommendations and stated its intent to address them.

- In both fiscal years 2012 and 2013, HHS reported over $1 billion in estimated improper payments in grant programs. HHS's OIG determined that HHS did not comply with all requirements of the Improper Payments Elimination and Recovery Act of 2010 for certain grant programs. HHS reported that it has steps planned and under way to help prevent and reduce improper payments.

OMB Circular No. A-123 notes that agency managers and staff should be encouraged to identify control deficiencies, as this reflects positively on the agency's commitment to recognizing and addressing management problems. Financial statement auditors, OIGs, and GAO continue to focus on grants internal controls through their audits and reviews, and the agencies continue to use the results of these reviews and their own assessments to develop corrective actions and oversee internal controls of federal grants to ensure that necessary controls are in place and operating effectively.

* * *

July 30, 2014

The Honorable Tom Carper
Chairman

The Honorable Tom Coburn, M.D.
Ranking Member
Committee on Homeland Security and Governmental Affairs
United States Senate

The Honorable Claire McCaskill
Chairman
Subcommittee on Financial and Contracting Oversight Committee on Homeland Security and Governmental Affairs
United States Senate

Federal grants are a significant tool for helping to achieve national objectives as they fund many programs important to the public.[1] In fiscal year 2013, the federal government obligated over $555 billion for grants for a wide array of activities, including building highways, bridges, and mass transit systems; hiring teachers and increasing student access to higher education;

funding medical and other types of research; and providing medical services, nutrition programs, and housing assistance for the economically disadvantaged.[2] Effective financial and management controls, also known as internal controls, are important for providing reasonable assurance to federal managers and taxpayers that grants are awarded properly, recipients are eligible, and federal grant funds are used as intended and in accordance with applicable laws and regulations. In numerous reviews over the years, we and agency Offices of Inspector General (OIG) have reported weaknesses in agencies' internal controls for managing and overseeing grants. (See the Related GAO Products list at the end of this report.)

Because of concerns about reported weaknesses in grants management and oversight across federal agencies, you asked us to review internal control issues over grants. This report (1) examines whether the five largest grant-making agencies' internal control oversight processes for their grant programs were consistent with Office of Management and Budget (OMB) requirements and (2) describes internal control issues that have been reported related to the grants management process and key grant programs. According to fiscal year 2012 USAspending.gov data, the most current available data at the time we started our review, the five largest grant-making agencies by grant dollars obligated were the Departments of Health and Human Services (HHS), Education (Education), Transportation (DOT), Agriculture (USDA), and Housing and Urban Development (HUD), which we selected as the subjects of our review.[3]

Using fiscal year 2012 USAspending.gov data, we selected 2 or 3 of the largest program offices in each of the five agencies, for a total of 12 program offices, so that our review would cover a large portion of the federal funds awarded for grants.[4] Although Medicaid, an HHS grant program, amounted to over 43 percent of the total obligations incurred for grants in fiscal year 2012, we elected to exclude the Medicaid grant program from our review because it has been the subject of numerous reviews, including many by GAO and HHS's OIG. Further, by doing so, we were able to include HHS programs that otherwise would not have been covered in our review and still comply with our selection criteria to cover over 80 percent of an agency's grant obligations, excluding Medicaid obligations. Thus our scope covers oversight of internal controls over a large percentage of the non-Medicaid federal grant dollars.

To assess the reliability of the USAspending.gov obligations data, we (1) reviewed recent GAO work that used the data and (2) compared results of ranking agencies by obligation amounts to the results of ranking agencies based on outlay amounts reported by OMB. [5] In our recent work, we had assessed the reliability of USAspending.gov obligations data for a report we issued in September 2012 by (1) performing electronic testing of required data elements, (2) reviewing existing information about the data and the system that produced them, and (3) interviewing agency officials knowledgeable about the data, and we determined that the data were sufficiently reliable for the purposes of that report. We also determined that the data were sufficiently reliable for the purpose of selecting agencies and program offices to review for this report. Further, to assess the reasonableness of our decision to use USAspending.gov obligations data to select the top five grant-making agencies, we reviewed OMB's Historical Table 12.3, Total Outlays for Grants to State and Local Governments, by Function, Agency and Program: 1940-2013, to determine the five largest grant-making agencies based on outlays for grants.[6] We reviewed and summarized the data and found that the same five agencies we selected based on USAspending.gov data were also the top five grant-making agencies according to OMB's data. As the OMB budget data had undergone rigorous review by OMB, we considered it sufficiently reliable for the purposes of this report.[7] See appendix I for information about our selection of program offices and further details on our scope and methodology.

To examine whether the agencies' internal control oversight processes for their grant programs were consistent with OMB requirements, we focused on the fiscal year 2012 internal control evaluation processes they performed to comply with the internal control assessment and reporting requirements of OMB Circular No. A-123 and its Appendix A.[8] We reviewed documentation of the OMB Circular No. A-123 internal control assessment processes for the selected program offices in the five agencies, including documentation of deficiencies identified and planned corrective actions. We interviewed agency officials and officials in the agencies' OIGs about the agencies' assessment processes and oversight of grants-related internal controls. We based our evaluation on OMB Circular No. A-123 and *Standards for Internal Control in the Federal Government*, specifically the standard for monitoring.[9]

To identify internal control issues that have been reported related to the grants management process and key grant programs, we reviewed the agencies' financial statement audit reports for fiscal years 2012 and 2013, and relevant GAO and OIG reports issued in fiscal years 2012 and 2013. We also reviewed improper payments information reported by the agencies in their fiscal year 2012 and 2013 agency financial reports and the results of the OIGs' reviews of agencies' compliance with improper payments laws. Finally, we reviewed management challenges reported by the agencies' OIGs. Appendix I provides details of our scope and methodology.

We conducted this performance audit from November 2012 to July 2014 in accordance with generally accepted government auditing standards. Those standards require that we plan and perform the audit to obtain sufficient, appropriate evidence to provide a reasonable basis for our findings and conclusions based on our audit objectives. We believe that the evidence obtained provides a reasonable basis for our findings and conclusions based on our audit objectives.

BACKGROUND

Grant Types and Programs

The federal government uses grants—forms of federal financial assistance to a state, a local government, or a nongovernmental recipient authorized to receive U.S. government assistance (e.g., charitable or educational institutions) for a specified public purpose—to achieve national objectives and respond to emerging trends, such as changing demographics and changing threats to homeland security. Federal grant programs are diverse and can vary in numerous ways including type, size, nature of recipients, and types of programs they fund. Grant programs also vary in the amount of discretion they give to the recipient in how the funds will be used and the way the funds are allocated or awarded. The types of grants awarded by the agencies in our review include the following:

- Block grants allow recipients, predominately states, to fund a broad range of activities within more general policy areas, such as community development or law enforcement.
- Formula grants are awarded to all eligible grantees based on a statutory allocation formula, which may be based on a number of variables, including population, poverty rate in a given area, or tax effort. The grants are typically awarded to states, which often pass funds through to eligible local government agencies and nonprofit organizations.
- Project grants are generally awarded on a competitive basis and provide funding for fixed or known periods for specific projects or the delivery of specific services or products. Project grants can include fellowships, scholarships, research grants, training grants,

traineeships, experimental and demonstration grants, evaluation grants, planning grants, technical assistance grants, survey grants, and construction grants.

These categories are not mutually exclusive and can overlap when used to define grant programs. For example, HUD awards Community Development Block Grant funds to states using a formula, and then the states distribute the funds to localities, sometimes as project grants.

Some agencies also use cooperative agreements, another form of financial assistance similar to grants, but one in which the federal agency is more involved with the recipient in implementing the financial assistance program. The distinguishing factor between a grant and a cooperative agreement is the degree of federal participation or involvement during the performance of the work activities.

Program Offices and Grant Programs in Our Review

Most of the program offices included in our review oversee and monitor large block and formula grant programs, while others award and manage numerous project or other smaller grants, as described in table 1.[10]

Table 1. Grant Program Offices Included in Our Review and Their Largest Grant Programs

Department and program office	Description
Department of Health and Human Services	
• Administration for Children and Families (ACF)	ACF's Temporary Assistance for Needy Families program awards block grants to statesto help needy families achieve self-sufficiency.
• National Institutes of Health (NIH)	NIH does not administer a specific large grant program; rather it awards and manages anumber of project grants for medical research.
• Centers for Medicare & Medicaid Services (CMS).	The Children's Health Insurance Program is the second largest grant program within CMS.[a]It is a formula grant program funded and administered jointly by CMS and the states.
Department of Education	
• Federal Student Aid (FSA)	FSA's Pell Grant Program provides need-based grants to low-income undergraduate and certain postbaccalaureate students to promote access to postsecondary education.

Department and program office	Description
• Office of Elementary and Secondary Education (OESE)	OESE's Title I grants program to state educational agencies provides financial assistance through formula grants to local educational agencies and schools with high numbers or high percentages of children from low-income families to help ensure that allchildren meet challenging state academic standards.
• Office of Special Education andRehabilitative Services (OSERS)	OSERS's Individuals with Disabilities Education Act, Part B Grants to States program provides formula grants to assist the 50 states, the District of Columbia, Puerto Rico, Outlying Areas, and the Freely Associated States in meeting the excess costs of providing special education and related services to children with disabilities.
Department of Transportation	
• Federal Highway Administration (FHWA)	FHWA's major grant program is Highway Planning and Construction, a formula grant program that provides funds to state departments of transportation.
• Federal Transit Administration (FTA)	FTA's major grant program is the Urbanized Area Formula Program, which provides funds through formula grants to public entities in urbanized areas to support transportation services.
Department of Agriculture	
• Food and Nutrition Service (FNS)	FNS's largest grant program is the National School Lunch Program, which consists of formula grants to state agencies to reimburse schools for lunches served to low-income children.
• National Institute of Food and Agriculture (NIFA)	NIFA does not administer a specific large grant program; rather, it provides a number of formula grants to land-grant universities and competitive grants to researchers in land-grant and other universities for research and education.
Department of Housing and Urban Development	
• Office of Community Planning and Development (CPD)	The largest grant program in CPD is the Community Development Block Grant program,which provides annual grants on a formula basis to general units of local government and states to ensure decent affordable housing, provide services to the most vulnerable in our communities, and create jobs through the expansion and retention of businesses.
• Office of Public and Indian Housing (PIH)	The largest grant program in PIH, the Public Housing Operating Fund, provides funds to public housing authorities through formula grants for the operation and management of public housing.

Source: GAO analysis of USAspending.gov data and agency information. | GAO-14-539.

[a] Medicaid is CMS's (and the federal government's) largest grant program, accounting for over 43 percent of all federal grant obligations in fiscal year 2012. We elected to exclude Medicaid from our review because it has been the subject of numerous reviews, including many by us and HHS's OIG. Further, by doing so, we were able to include HHS grant programs that otherwise would not have been covered in our review and still comply with our selection criteria to cover over 80 percent of an agency's grant obligations, excluding Medicaid.

Importance of Internal Control

At all stages of the grants life cycle, it is essential that effective internal control systems are in place. Internal control represents an agency's plans, methods, and procedures used to meet its mission, goals, and objectives and serves as the first line of defense in safeguarding assets and preventing and detecting errors, fraud, waste, abuse, and mismanagement. Effective oversight of internal controls for grant programs is important to provide reasonable assurance to taxpayers that grants are awarded properly, recipients are eligible, and federal funds are used as intended and in accordance with applicable laws and regulations. The term reasonable assurance is important because no matter how well-designed and well-operated, internal control cannot provide absolute assurance that agency objectives will be met. Cost-benefit is an important concept to internal control considerations. Internal control is very broad and encompasses all controls within an agency, covering an agency's entire mission and operations, not just financial operations. Figure 1 shows examples of agencies' control activities in each phase of the grants life cycle.

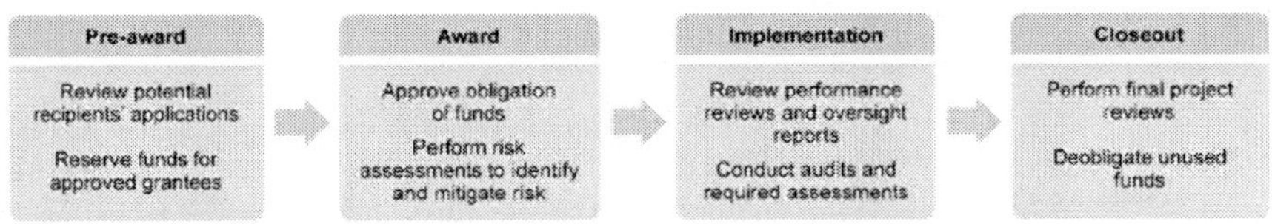

Source: GAO analysis of agencies' internal control documentation. | GAO-14-539.

Figure 1. Internal Control Activities through the Grants Life Cycle.

Congress passed the Federal Managers' Financial Integrity Act (FMFIA)[11] to help improve the management of federal government programs and strengthen agency internal control systems by requiring ongoing evaluations and reports on the adequacy of executive agency internal control systems.[12] FMFIA, as implemented by GAO standards and OMB guidance, requires agency managers to establish internal control systems that provide reasonable assurance regarding the agency's proper use of funds and resources, compliance with statutes and regulations, and preparation of reliable financial reports. In accordance with FMFIA, OMB has established guidance for agencies for evaluating and reporting on their internal controls. This guidance is now contained in OMB Circular No. A-123, *Management's Responsibility for Internal Control.* FMFIA also requires GAO to issue internal control standards for the federal government, which are now contained in *Standards for Internal Control in the Federal Government.*[13] These standards provide the overall framework for establishing and maintaining internal control and for identifying and addressing major performance and management challenges and areas at greatest risk of fraud, waste, abuse, and mismanagement. The standards also provide that for internal control to be effective, an agency's management should establish both a supportive overall control environment and specific control activities directed at carrying out the agency's objectives.

Annual Internal Control Assessment and Reporting

OMB Circular No. A-123 states that management is responsible for establishing and maintaining internal control to achieve the objectives of effective and efficient operations, reliable financial reporting, and compliance with applicable laws and regulations. OMB Circular No. A-123 provides guidance to federal managers on improving the accountability and effectiveness of federal programs and operations by establishing, assessing, correcting, and reporting on internal control. OMB Circular No. A-123 requires federal agencies and managers to take systematic and proactive measures to, among other things, assess the adequacy of internal control in federal programs and operations and report annually on internal control through management assurance statements.

To assess the adequacy of internal controls, federal agencies conduct an annual assessment that includes testing key controls, identifying needed improvements, and developing and implementing corrective action plans. As part of this assessment, OMB Circular No. A-123 states that management should consider a variety of internal and external sources, including management knowledge and internal program reviews, financial statement audit reports, single audit reports, and improper payment reviews and reports. Further, OMB Circular No. A-123 provides that the agency head should consider input from senior program officials and the OIG.

OMB Circular No. A-123 requires management to annually provide assurances about the adequacy and effectiveness of its internal control in a management assurance statement. This statement of assurance, which is included in an agency's performance and accountability report or agency financial report, represents the agency head's informed judgment as to the overall adequacy and effectiveness of internal control within the agency based on management's assessment as described above, including the consideration of outside sources such as the results of financial statement audits. Management will give an unqualified statement of assurance when there are no material weaknesses to report and will give a qualified statement of assurance when there are material weaknesses related to internal control.[14]

Other Mechanisms for Overseeing and Monitoring Grant Program Internal Controls

Federal agencies, including the five in our review, use other mechanisms and processes, in addition to OMB Circular No. A-123, to oversee and monitor their grants internal controls. The single audit—audit of federal awards, including grant funds, administered by state and local governments and nonprofit organizations—is intended to be an important mechanism used by federal agencies to ensure accountability for federal funds.[15] Single audit reports provide information about the validity of grant expenditures, adequacy of internal controls over federal funds, compliance with grant rules and regulations, and questioned amounts. Grant-making agencies use single audit reports to monitor grantees' compliance with program and financial requirements. The agencies also use other mechanisms to monitor their grant programs, for example, creating annual grant performance plans, performing eligibility determinations, reviewing grantee financial reports, and conducting management control reviews.

Improper Payments

Congress passed three successive acts from 2002 to 2013 toward eliminating improper payments.[16] The Improper Payments Information Act of 2002 (IPIA) required executive branch agencies to annually review all programs and activities to identify those that are susceptible to significant improper payments, to estimate the annual amount of improper payments for such programs and activities, and to report these estimates along with actions taken to reduce improper payments for programs with estimates that exceed $10 million.[17] This act was subsequently amended by the Improper Payments Elimination and Recovery Act of 2010 (IPERA), which expanded on the previous requirements for identifying, estimating, and reporting on programs and activities susceptible to significant improper payments and for recovering overpayments across a broad range of federal programs.[18] On January 10, 2013, the Improper Payments Elimination and Recovery Improvement Act of 2012 was enacted to impose further requirements to identify, prevent, and recover payment errors.[19]

IPERA requires that OIGs determine whether their agencies are in compliance with the criteria listed in IPERA and annually report the results to the head of the agency, among others. OMB also plays a key role in the oversight of the government-wide improper payments issue.[20] OMB has established guidance in Appendix C of OMB Circular No. A-123 to implement the requirements of IPERA.[21] IPERA and the OMB guidance require an OIG to use the following criteria in making a compliance determination on whether the agency has

- published the agency financial report and OMB-required accompanying information on the agency's website,
- conducted a risk assessment for specific programs to determine whether they are susceptible to significant improper payments,
- published improper payment estimates for all high-risk programs,
- reported on actions to reduce improper payments,
- published and met targets for reducing improper payments,
- reported a gross improper payment rate of less than 10 percent for each high-risk program, and
- reported efforts to recapture improper payments.

For the period within the scope of this report, IPERA defined significant improper payments as those in any particular program or activity that exceed both 2.5 percent of program or activity payments and $10 million annually or that exceed $100 million.[22] For each program identified as susceptible and determined to be at risk of improper payments, agencies are required to report to the President and Congress the annual amount of estimated improper payments, along with steps taken and actions planned to reduce them. Agencies report this information in their annual performance and accountability report or agency financial report.

AGENCIES' ASSESSMENTS OF INTERNAL CONTROLS OVER GRANTS PROGRAMS WERE CONSISTENT WITH OMB REQUIREMENTS

The processes used by all five agencies to conduct their internal control assessments for fiscal year 2012 were consistent with the requirements in OMB Circular No. A-123. The agencies identified areas of risk in which to implement key controls and then monitored and tested those controls. The agencies identified deficiencies through the control tests, prepared and implemented corrective action plans to address the deficiencies identified, and reported on their internal control through management assurance statements.

Agencies Identified Significant Grants Programs and Processes to Include in Their Fiscal Year 2012 Internal Control Assessments

OMB Circular No. A-123 requires that agencies identify significant areas within their operations in which to implement key controls and then continuously monitor and test those controls. All five agencies conducted a risk assessment to identify significant processes or programs to include in their internal control assessment processes for fiscal year 2012.

Table 2. Grants-Related Processes and Programs Selected for Internal Control Assessment in Fiscal Year 2012

Department and program office	Grants-related process and program selected for review
Department of Health and Human Services	
• Administration for Children and Families	Grants management
• National Institutes of Health	Grants management
• Centers for Medicare & Medicaid Services	Children's Health Insurance Programa
Department of Education	
• Federal Student Aid	Pell Grant Program Operations Student Eligibility/Application Processing School Eligibility Service Group Processes
• Office of Elementary and Secondary Education	Grants management – process for ensuring grantees correct findingsresulting from monitoring activitiesb

Department and program office	Grants-related process and program selected for review
• Office of Special Education and Rehabilitative Services	Grants management – process for ensuring grantees correct findingsresulting from monitoring activitiesb
Department of Transportation	
• Federal Highway Administration	Grants management
• Federal Transit Administration	Grants management
Department of Agriculture	
• Food and Nutrition Service	Grants management/cooperative agreements
• National Institute of Food and Agriculture	Grants management/cooperative agreements
Department of Housing and Urban Development	
• Community Planning and Developmentc	Disaster Recovery Assistance Neighborhood Stabilization Program #1
• Office of Public and Indian Housing	Public Housing Operating Fund

Source: GAO analysis of agency data. | GAO-14-539.

[a] Medicaid, the largest federal grant program, is part of the Centers for Medicare & Medicaid Services. As discussed in app. I, we did not include Medicaid in our review.

[b] Based on the deficiencies identified in fiscal year 2011, the Department of Education determined its fiscal year 2012 OMB Circular No. A-123 assessment would focus on the process for ensuring grantee correction of findings resulting from monitoring activities, across multiple program offices, including the Offices of Elementary and Secondary Education and Special Education and Rehabilitative Services.

[c] Disaster Recovery Assistance and the Neighborhood Stabilization Program are program areas within the Community Development Block Grant program.

Based on these risk assessments, as shown in table 2, each agency selected its grants management process (or parts of its grants management process) or it selected grant programs to test controls as part of its fiscal year 2012 OMB Circular No. A-123 internal control assessment process.[23] OMB Circular No. A-123 does not specify a recommended approach for evaluating or testing controls for processes or programs. When conducting these risk assessments, the agencies considered the effect that various factors could have on the risk that program objectives may not be met or a misstatement may be made in the financial statements. OMB Circular No. A-123 does not include requirements regarding specific factors to consider when determining which controls to test, and the agencies differed in the number of and specific risk factors they considered, as shown in table 3. Management at all of the agencies approved the selection of processes or programs to be included in their agencies' internal control assessments.

Table 3. Factors Considered by the Five Largest Grant-Making Agencies When Determining the Controls to Test for Their Annual Internal Control Assessments

			Five largest grant-making agencies		
Factors	*Department of Health and Human Services*	*Department of Education*	*Department of Transportation*	*Department of Agriculture*	*Department of Housing and Urban Development*
Impact on mission; vision and sensitivity	√		√		
Prior year findings or known issues	√	√	√	√	
Included in prior year A-123 review		√	√	√	√
Nature or complexity of process	√	√	√	√	
Human capital	√	√		√	
New or significantly changed programs or operations	√	√		√	
Fraud, waste, and abuse	√	√	√	√	
Material to financial reporting	√	√	√	√	√

Source: GAO analysis of agency documentation. | GAO-14-539.

Agencies Identified Grants Internal Control Issues and Developed Corrective Action Plans

OMB Circular No. A-123 requires agencies to identify needed improvements in controls and take corresponding corrective actions. It also notes that agency managers and staff should be encouraged to identify control deficiencies, as this reflects positively on the agency's commitment to recognizing and addressing management problems. Further, *Standards for Internal Control in the Federal Government* states that findings of audits and other reviews should be promptly resolved.[24] The agencies identified deficiencies in certain grants internal controls as a result of their fiscal year 2012 OMB Circular No. A-123 assessment processes. When agencies identified control deficiencies, they prepared corrective action plans that included steps to be taken, responsible parties, and timeframes for completion. We reviewed these plans and determined that if implemented effectively, the steps to be taken should correct the deficiencies. For example:

- HHS's Administration for Children and Families tested controls for the grants management process and identified deficiencies that contributed to delays in receiving grantee financial reports and resolving single audit findings. The Administration for Children and Families developed and implemented corrective actions, including following up with and providing assistance to grantees to improve the timeliness of periodic reporting and taking steps to ensure proper approvals and signatures on documents related to addressing single audit findings.
- HHS's National Institutes of Health tested controls for the grants management process and found deficiencies in following up with grantees regarding their late filing of financial reports during the grant closeout phase and resolution of single audit findings. The National Institutes of Health prepared a corrective action plan that includes procedures to improve the timeliness of grantee reports and actions to improve instructions to grantees regarding repayment of disallowed funds found in single audits. It plans to complete these actions by December 2014.
- Education's Internal Controls Evaluation Group (Evaluation Group) in the Office of the Chief Financial Officer tested related controls for discretionary and formula grants across several program offices, including the Office of Elementary and Secondary Education and Office of Special Education and Rehabilitative Services, and identified deficiencies. Some controls were found to be deficient primarily because of a lack of documentation. The deficiencies resulted in two findings in various offices, including the Office of Elementary and Secondary Education. According to the Evaluation Group, the Office of Elementary and Secondary Education

implemented corrective actions, which included ensuring that grantees are making progress on their noncompliance issues before being awarded additional grant funds and providing technical assistance to grantees to help them successfully carry out their projects.

- DOT's Federal Transit Administration identified a deficiency related to tracking single audit findings. The findings were not being entered into the automated system used to manage oversight program activities and were being tracked offline. The Federal Transit Administration implemented its corrective action plan by issuing a memo to regional offices reiterating the requirements to enter single audit findings in the system in a timely manner and holding routine conference calls and training sessions with regional offices about the issue. Also, according to the Federal Transit Administration, it updated the standard operating procedures for single audit findings, which were in the agency's review process as of April 2014.
- USDA's Food and Nutrition Service and its National Institute of Food and Agriculture tested controls for the grants management process and identified deficiencies related to grant accruals, completion of site visit reports, and review of single audits. For example, the National Institute of Food and Agriculture identified a deficiency in the control related to timely review and resolution of single audits. Its corrective action plan included drafting standard operating procedures; developing a single audit tracking spreadsheet to document open reviews, findings, and timelines; and obtaining contractor assistance to help clear the extensive backlog of single audit reviews. As of February 2014, according to the National Institute of Food and Agriculture, the backlog was being addressed.
- HUD's Office of Community Planning and Development assessed controls for the Neighborhood Stabilization Program and identified a deficiency related to the timeliness of grantee reports used to monitor grantees. In response to the finding, a corrective action plan was created to address the untimely filing of these reports. According to HUD, the Office of Community Planning and Development solicited and received recommendations from field offices for improvements to the process. The field office feedback is being incorporated into guidance, and the Office of Community Planning and Development plans to communicate the updated guidance to field offices no later than June 30, 2014.

Agencies Reported on Their Internal Control Assessments in Management Assurance Statements

OMB Circular No. A-123 requires agencies to report annually on management's judgment regarding the adequacy and effectiveness of internal control in assurance statements signed by management. All five agencies included management assurance statements in their annual agency financial reports, as required. Based on their fiscal year 2012 OMB Circular No. A-123 assessment processes, which included testing of key program and process controls, results of financial statement audits, and other information, all five agencies gave a qualified statement of assurance for fiscal year 2012.[25]

- Three of the five agencies (HHS, DOT, and USDA) qualified their assurance statements because of weaknesses in grants processes or grants programs. Specifically, HHS and USDA reported material weaknesses because of noncompliance with IPERA for some large grant programs, which is discussed later in this report. DOT reported a material weakness involving unliquidated obligations, including in grant programs.26 These weaknesses were also identified by financial statement auditors, as discussed later in this report.
- HUD and Education qualified their fiscal year 2012 assurance for reasons not directly related to grants. HUD qualified its assurance because of weaknesses in its human capital operations, and Education qualified its assurance because of weaknesses in its servicing systems for student loan programs.

INTERNAL CONTROL ISSUES REPORTED INCLUDE CONTROL DEFICIENCIES, IMPROPER PAYMENTS, AND MANAGEMENT CHALLENGES

In addition to the issues identified through the OMB Circular No. A-123 process, other audits and reviews have reported internal control issues related to the grants management process and grant programs. We examined the agencies' financial statement audit reports and other reports issued by GAO and the agencies' OIGs and found that internal control deficiencies related to grants, including weaknesses in controls for monitoring and oversight of grantees and unliquidated grant obligations and certain accounting methods for grant programs, have been reported. Further, some of the agencies identified and reported on improper payments in grants programs, and OIGs for some of the agencies reported issues related to agencies' improper payments information. OIGs have also reported management challenges related to grants.

Financial Statement Auditors Reported Significant Deficiencies in Controls over Grants Programs

The primary purpose of a financial statement audit is to provide an opinion about whether an entity's financial statements are presented fairly in all material respects in conformity with an applicable financial reporting framework. Reporting on financial statement audits also includes reports on internal control over financial reporting and on compliance with provisions of laws, regulations, contracts, and grant agreements that have a material effect on the financial statements. Financial statement auditors for three of the agencies reported deficiencies in grants monitoring controls and grants accounting methods.

Specifically, for fiscal years 2012 and 2013, financial statement auditors for DOT, USDA, and HUD reported significant deficiencies, some of which were considered to be material weaknesses, in the agencies' internal controls associated with grant programs.[27] Reported grants-related deficiencies primarily related to accounting for grant programs and monitoring procedures over grant activities. A common issue at many agencies is deficiencies in controls over unliquidated grants obligations. Financial statement auditors at DOT, USDA, and HUD reported such deficiencies, as discussed below, and we have previously reported on the issue. In April 2012, we reported that millions of dollars of grant obligations remain in expired grant accounts—accounts that were more than 3 months past the grant end date and had no activity for 9 months or more.[28] Agency regulations typically impose closeout procedures upon both the awarding agency and the grantee. Generally, within 90 days after the completion of the grant award, grantees must submit all financial, performance, and other reports as required by the terms and conditions of the award. Also within this 90-day period, grantees generally are to liquidate all obligations incurred under the award. These closeout procedures make funds less susceptible to fraud, waste, and mismanagement; reduce the potential costs to agencies for fees paid to maintain grant accounts; and may enable agencies to redirect resources to other projects.

DOT's financial statement auditors reported deficiencies related to unliquidated obligations in grants programs for both fiscal years 2012 and 2013 and controls over grant accruals in fiscal year 2012.

- In fiscal year 2012, the auditors reported a material weakness related to controls over the review and monitoring of grant and nongrant unliquidated obligations, including those at the Federal Highway Administration and the Federal Transit Administration. Specifically, the Federal Highway Administration and the Federal Transit Administration did not timely identify and deobligate unused obligation balances. DOT subsequently performed the necessary deobligations to correct its financial data. Further, to correct the underlying cause, the Federal Highway Administration and the Federal Transit Administration revised their procedures for reviewing and addressing unliquidated obligations in February 2013 and May 2013, respectively. In fiscal year 2013, while the auditors continued to identify issues with unused obligations, they no longer considered the issue a material weakness and reduced it to a significant deficiency.
- In fiscal year 2012, the auditors reported a significant deficiency related to controls over grant accruals at some program offices, including the Federal Highway Administration. At fiscal year-end, DOT calculated and recorded an estimated liability for amounts owed to its grantees for costs incurred under grant agreements but not yet billed to or reimbursed by DOT. The auditors reported that the Federal Highway Administration did not have adequate controls in place to ensure that all significant grantees and grant programs were properly included in DOT's grant accrual estimate methodology, and as a result, the grant accruals were potentially understated. This issue was no longer reported as a significant deficiency in fiscal year 2013.

For fiscal years 2012 and 2013, USDA financial statement auditors reported a significant deficiency involving unliquidated obligations. They reported that ineffective monitoring and reviewing resulted in invalid obligations remaining open, thus restricting the availability of funding authority and increasing the risk of misstating obligations as of year-end. In the fiscal year 2012 audit report, the auditors noted that substantial improvements had been made to effectively monitor and review unliquidated obligations since fiscal year 2011, when the auditors reported this issue as a material weakness. The auditors made no new related recommendations in the fiscal year 2012 report and downgraded the material weakness to a significant deficiency. In the fiscal year 2013 audit report, the auditors again reported the issue as a significant deficiency and recommended that the department emphasize the importance of complying with USDA's requirements related to unliquidated obligations. The auditors also noted that USDA management reported that the Forest Service was not in compliance with certain federal requirements related to managing grants programs in fiscal years 2012 and 2013.[29]

HUD's financial statement auditors reported significant deficiencies related to controls over unliquidated obligations and controls for monitoring some grant programs for fiscal years 2012 and 2013. In addition, the auditors reported a material weakness caused by HUD's noncompliance with the Federal Financial Management Improvement Act of 1996 (FFMIA), including noncompliance associated with the Office of Community Planning and Development's information systems for fiscal years 2012 and 2013.[30]

- During the financial statement audits for fiscal years 2012 and 2013, HUD's financial statement auditors reported a significant deficiency related to unliquidated obligations. The auditors found inadequate procedures related to timely reviews and recapture of unexpended obligations for several grant programs, including those within the Office of Community Planning and Development, which led to misstatements in HUD's obligation balances. In the fiscal year 2013 audit report, the auditors reported that review and closeout policies had been drafted but not finalized or implemented because of competing priorities. The auditors recommended that the Office of Community Planning and Development review and deobligate invalid obligations.
- For fiscal year 2012, the auditors reported a significant deficiency related to the Office of Community Planning and Development's controls for monitoring grantees, including that the system used to communicate the results and status of on-site monitoring was not effective because field offices did not always follow the monitoring handbook and did not always update the information system to reflect current status of monitoring reviews. The auditors repeated recommendations from the prior year to ensure that the monitoring handbook is followed, the information in the grants management system is accurate, and findings from grantee reviews are closed and funds are collected. By fiscal year 2013, most of the recommendations

had been implemented, and the auditors no longer reported this issue as a significant deficiency for fiscal year 2013.

- The auditors reported material weaknesses for fiscal years 2012 and 2013 because HUD's financial management systems did not comply with FFMIA, including noncompliance associated with the Office of Community Planning and Development's information systems. The material weakness was due, in part, to the Office of Community Planning and Development's method of accounting and the system used for disbursing obligations, which did not comply with the requirements of FFMIA for maintaining financial management systems that substantially comply with federal financial management systems requirements and applicable federal accounting standards. The auditors reported that the Office of Community Planning and Development was taking steps to address the issues.

Because of many of these internal control issues and ones identified at other federal agencies, we reported a significant deficiency in internal controls related to grants management in our audit reports on the U.S. government's consolidated financial statements for fiscal years 2012 and 2013.[31] Deficiencies in grants management internal controls could adversely affect the federal government's ability to ensure that grant funds are being properly reported and used in accordance with applicable program laws and regulations.

In addition to reporting on deficiencies in internal controls, financial statement auditors also report on instances of noncompliance with certain laws and regulations. Auditors for HHS and USDA reported instances of noncompliance with IPERA for some grant programs for fiscal years 2012 and 2013, which are discussed later in this report.

GAO and OIGs Reported Issues Related to Grants Monitoring and Other Aspects of Grant Programs

We and agency OIGs have reviewed federal grants programs and reported findings and recommendations related to monitoring and other aspects of grant programs at many federal agencies, including the five in our review. For example:

- In December 2012, we reported on HHS's Administration for Children and Families Temporary Assistance for Needy Families program.[32] We found that the Temporary Assistance for Needy Families program's accountability framework provided incomplete information on how states' noncash services were contributing to the program's purposes. States are required to submit several reports to HHS. Taken together, these reports serve as the accountability framework in place to help HHS and Congress ensure that states use Temporary Assistance for Needy Families program funds for proper purposes and identify needed program improvements. We recommended that HHS develop a detailed plan with timelines to revise reporting categories for program expenditures. HHS formed an internal workgroup to review and revise a Temporary Assistance for Needy Families program reporting form for collecting more-detailed expenditure data, and published two *Federal Register* notices in September 2013 and January 2014, regarding proposed revisions to the financial reporting form. HHS plans to issue the form effective for fiscal year 2015.

- In June 2011, we reported on education reform grants to states required by the American Recovery and Reinvestment Act of 2009 (Recovery Act).[33] We found that Education had provided extensive support to grantee states and had begun monitoring states' progress in meeting program goals.[34] Education also developed ways for grantees to share information, such as hosting meetings on specific initiatives. Some officials from grantee states said they would find this information useful, but they were generally unaware of these resources or were unable to access them. We recommended that Education facilitate information sharing among grantees. Among other things, Education established communities of practice to address multiple topics. Education oversees the activities of each community by managing a work plan that includes the target dates for each activity. In addition, Education communicates these activities to members of each community of practice via emails and calls as well as a monthly update to all grantees with upcoming dates and events.
- In December 2011, HHS's OIG reported on a science awards program at the National Institutes of Health.[35] The program is administered through cooperative agreements, which are similar to grants but require more involvement by the awarding agency. The OIG reported that it found documentation and reporting issues, which the National Institutes of Health is taking steps to correct. Specifically, the Clinical and Translational Science Awards Program did not properly document

awardees' progress under their cooperative agreements. The OIG recommended that the National Institutes of Health ensure that program staff document their monitoring of awardee progress; ensure timely submission of required reports; maintain official files in accordance with federal policy; and, as required for cooperative agreements, provide substantial involvement to Clinical and Translational Science Awards Program awardees. The National Institutes of Health concurred with the recommendations and stated that it had taken or planned to take steps to implement them.

- In August 2012, DOT's OIG reported on weaknesses in grants oversight at the Federal Transit Administration and made several related recommendations.[36] Specifically, the OIG reported that the Federal Transit Administration lacked adequate guidance for ensuring that findings from grantee oversight reviews were consistently identified and adequately tracked to ensure grantees were complying with laws and regulations and implementing corrective actions. In response, the Federal Transit Administration stated that it was revising its oversight and review processes to, among other things, identify grant recipients needing technical assistance and developing standard operating procedures to provide more consistency across regions and implementing new performance measures. The OIG reported that these actions, both those taken and planned, were responsive to the recommendations.
- In February 2012, USDA's OIG performed work related to the Recovery Act and reported that it found that the Food and Nutrition Service did not create adequate, proactive controls to ensure that states awarded grants for schools to purchase and renovate food service equipment based on Recovery Act criteria, and did not ensure timely reporting of Recovery Act spending data on Recovery.gov as required by OMB guidance on using funds pursuant to the Recovery Act.[37] The OIG recommended that the Food and Nutrition Service continue to update and implement adequate, proactive controls for its standard competitive grant award process. The Food and Nutrition Service agreed that continuous improvement of controls over the competitive award process was warranted and agreed with the OIG's recommendation to update controls. According to USDA's Office of the Chief Financial Officer, the Food and Nutrition Service took corrective action and the recommendation was closed in February 2013.

- In July 2013, HUD's OIG reported that HUD's guidance for ensuring grantee compliance with the Community Development Block Grant program's timeliness spending requirement was not always implemented effectively, and documentation of HUD's rationale for not sanctioning noncompliant grantees was inadequate. [38] HUD is to annually determine whether Community Development Block Grant grantees—states, cities, and counties—are carrying out grant activities in a timely manner, which includes timely drawdown of grant funds. HUD is to generate a monthly report to help field offices monitor grantees' compliance with the timeliness spending requirement. The OIG recommended, among other things, that HUD (1) strengthen controls over Community Development Block Grant procedures related to the monthly timeliness report and notification to noncompliant grantees and (2) establish documentation requirements and procedures for grantees that do not comply with the timeliness spending requirement. HUD generally concurred with these recommendations and stated that it would enhance current procedures to address the recommendations.

Agencies Reported Improper Payments in Grant Programs

In both fiscal years 2012 and 2013, four of the largest grant-making agencies reported almost $5 billion in estimated improper payments in grants programs. Agencies are required by IPIA, as amended by IPERA and implemented by OMB guidance, to periodically review and assess all programs and activities to identify those susceptible to significant improper payments, estimate the annual amount of improper payments, and report these estimates along with actions taken to reduce improper payments when the estimates exceed both $10 million annually and 2.5 percent of program or activity payments (or 1.5 percent of program or activity payments starting in fiscal year 2014) or when the estimates exceed $100 million.

As shown in table 4, four of the agencies reported improper payment estimates and error rates (i.e., amount of estimated improper payments divided by total program outlays) in grant programs administered by the program offices in our review for fiscal years 2012 and 2013.[39]

Table 4. Improper Payment Estimates and Error Rates in Grant Programs, Fiscal Years 2012 and 2013

Dollars in millions				
	Fiscal year 2012		*Fiscal year 2013*	
Department and grant program	*Improper payments*	*Error rate (percentages)*	*Improper payments*	*Error rate(percentages)*
Department of Health and Human Services (HHS)				
• Head Start	$46.2	0.6	a	a
• Foster Care	80.2	6.2	$70.0	5.3
• Child Care and Development Funds	474	9.2	306.0	5.9
• Children's Health Insurance Program	704	8.2	646	7.1
Department of Education (Education)				
• Pell Grants	829	2.5	731	2.3
Department and grant program	*Improper payments*	*Error rate (percentages)*	*Improper payments*	*Error rate(percentages)*
• Title I Grants	28.3	0.2	56.7	0.4
Department of Transportation (DOT)				
• Planning and Construction	103.2	0.2	91.4	0.2
• Formula Grants	38.1	0.4	62.6	0.7
Department of Agriculture (USDA)				
• School Lunch Program	1,557	15.5	1,774	15.7
• Special Supplemental Nutrition Program for Women, Infants, and Children	202	4.1	198	4.4
• School Breakfast Program	752	25.2	831	25.3
• Child and Adult Care Food Program	14	1.6	10	1.1

Source: Agency financial reports for fiscal years 2012 and 2013 for HHS, Education, DOT, and USDA. | GAO-14-539.

[a] According to HHS, OMB granted HHS relief from reporting annual error rate estimates for fiscal year 2013 because of Head Start's strong internal controls, monitoring systems, and low reported error rates.

OIGs Reported Issues with Agencies' Improper Payments Information

IPERA requires, among other things, OIGs to determine whether their agencies are in compliance with the criteria listed in IPERA and annually report the results to the heads of their agencies, the Comptroller General, and certain congressional committees. Many OIGs do so by reviewing their agencies' improper payment reporting in the annual agency financial report and accompanying materials. For fiscal years 2012 and 2013, the OIGs reported the following for their respective agencies.

- The HHS OIG reported that while HHS met many of IPERA's compliance requirements, it did not fully comply with IPERA for fiscal years 2012 and 2013 for some of its grant programs.[40] Specifically, the OIG reported that HHS did not comply with IPERA for the Children's Health Insurance Program for fiscal year 2012 because it did not publish a corrective action plan for the program's improper payments. HHS did publish a corrective action plan for this program for fiscal year 2013. For the Foster Care program, the OIG reported that HHS did not comply for fiscal year 2012 because the improper payment rate of 6.2 percent exceeded HHS's target rate of 4.5 percent. For fiscal year 2013, HHS's Foster Care improper payments rate of 5.3 percent met the target rate of 6 percent for that year. In the case of the Temporary Assistance for Needy Families program, the OIG reported that HHS did not report an improper payments estimate for either fiscal year 2012 or fiscal year 2013. According to HHS, statutory limitations related to obtaining state data prohibited HHS from developing an estimate. However, HHS has reported that is taking steps and has planned actions to help prevent and reduce improper payments, including providing technical assistance to help strengthen state program integrity efforts, revisions to the Temporary Assistance to Needy Families financial reporting form so that states can provide more accurate information about how they are using program funds, and sharing with states information and best practices for reducing improper payments.
- The USDA OIG reported that USDA did not meet IPERA's compliance requirements for fiscal years 2012 and 2013 for some of its grants programs, including the School Lunch and School Breakfast Programs and the Child and Adult Care Food Program.[41] The OIG

reported that the School Lunch and School Breakfast Programs did not comply because they reported improper payment rates that exceeded 10 percent for both fiscal years 2012 and 2013. According to the OIG, the Food and Nutrition Service's administration of these programs was highly decentralized and involved many governmental and nongovernmental organizations to provide benefits at approximately 100,000 locations. The OIG reported that Food and Nutrition Service officials stated that they were aware of the significant improper payment rate in these two programs, and they hired a contractor to conduct a study to help develop initiatives and practices to address this problem. The OIG reported that the results of the study were pending at the time of its review for fiscal year 2013 and noted that Food and Nutrition Service officials believed it would take time to achieve an error rate less than 10 percent.[42] For the Child and Adult Care Food Program, the OIG reported that USDA reported only a partial estimate of improper payments for both fiscal years 2012 and 2013 because the Food and Nutrition Service did not have a cost-effective method for estimating improper payments for one of the program's two components—Family Day Care Homes Meal Claims. Food and Nutrition Service officials continued to report difficulties in determining a gross estimate for the Child and Adult Care Food Program, which included over 190,000 participating day care homes and centers with varied eligibility requirements for each of the program's two components. According to the OIG's report on its fiscal year 2013 review, the Food and Nutrition Service has conducted feasibility studies since 2006 to develop a reliable method for estimating improper payments, but the studies were not reliable. The Food and Nutrition Service told us that it continues to assess methods of estimating erroneous payments and that a new study will be conducted in 2014 to explore an alternative method of measuring the rate of erroneous payments.

- For both fiscal years 2012 and 2013, Education's OIG reported that Education met IPERA's compliance requirements; however, improvements were needed in the estimation methodology for both the Pell Grant and Direct Loan Programs.[43] The OIG recommended that Education (1) continue working with OMB to obtain approval for an estimation methodology that addresses current limitations with some data used and (2) where estimates are based on the results of program reviews, include all program review results for a sufficient period of time in the universe of potential improper payments. Education agreed with the OIG's recommendations and noted that it had modified its fiscal year 2014 estimation methodologies.

- For fiscal years 2012 and 2013, DOT's OIG reported that although DOT met IPERA's compliance requirements, some of the information reported in its agency financial reports was inaccurate. 44 The OIG recommended, among other things, that DOT implement procedures to ensure that all elements required for IPERA reporting are accurate and supported by documentation. The OIG also reported that while DOT's programs met IPERA's required improper payment rate of less than 10 percent for both fiscal years 2012 and 2013, the Federal Transit Administration did not meet its target error rates for those years. In its 2012 and 2013 agency financial reports, DOT reported error rates of 0.44 percent and 0.73 percent, respectively, for its Formula Grants Program. These rates did not did not meet the target error rates reported in DOT's fiscal year 2012 and 2013 agency financial reports of 0.25 percent and 0.50 percent, respectively.

OIGs Reported Management Challenges Related to Grant Programs

The Reports Consolidation Act of 2000 requires each OIG to prepare a statement that summarizes what the OIG considers to be the most serious management and performance challenges facing its agency.[45] Agencies are to include the OIG's summary of management challenges in their annual agency financial report or performance and accountability report.

- HHS's OIG reported grants management and identifying and reducing improper payments as top grants-related management challenges for fiscal year 2012. HHS is the largest grant-making agency in the federal government, and oversight and management of both new and continuing grant programs are crucial to HHS's mission. The OIG has found internal control deficiencies, problems with financial stability, inadequate organizational structures, inadequate procurement and property management, and inadequate personnel policies and procedures among grantees. In addition, the OIG reported that HHS faces challenges complying with IPERA for some of its programs, including the Temporary Assistance for Needy Families program, as discussed above. For fiscal year 2013, the OIG reported a similar challenge for grants management—protecting HHS grants and contract funds from fraud, waste, and abuse. The improper payments-related challenge reported by the OIG for fiscal year 2013 was focused on Medicare programs and not on grants programs.

- Education's OIG reported management challenges for fiscal years 2012 and 2013, including oversight and monitoring of the department's programs and grantees and improper payments. Regarding oversight and monitoring, the OIG reported that the number of different entities and programs requiring monitoring and oversight, the amount of funding that flows through the department, and the impact that ineffective monitoring could have on stakeholders make monitoring and oversight a challenge. The OIG also reported that Education faces challenges in its efforts to successfully prevent, identify, and recapture improper payments in some programs, including the Pell Grant and Title I Programs. For fiscal year 2013, while the OIG noted progress was being made in some areas, it reported management challenges similar to those for fiscal year 2012.
- For fiscal year 2012, DOT's OIG reported a grants-related management challenge: ensuring effective oversight of Recovery Act projects and applying related lessons learned to improve DOT's infrastructure programs. For fiscal year 2013, the OIG reported challenges in strengthening existing highway and transit project oversight mechanisms and improving financial management over grants to better use funds, create jobs, and improve infrastructure.
- For fiscal years 2012 and 2013, USDA's OIG reported a management challenge: identifying, reporting, and reducing improper payments, including those in some grant programs. The OIG reported, among other things, that USDA continues to struggle to meet IPERA's compliance requirements for reporting and preventive measures. Also, the OIG noted that related quarterly reports did not always provide accurate, complete, and timely information.
- Among other issues, HUD's OIG reported oversight and monitoring of some of its grant programs as a management challenge in fiscal years 2012 and 2013. The challenges included oversight of Recovery Act funds and monitoring grants for housing assistance programs and for disaster recovery. For example, the OIG reported that HUD faces challenges in monitoring Community Development Block Grant

Disaster Recovery Assistance funds because of, among other things, limited resources for performing oversight, the broad nature of HUD projects, a lack of understanding of disaster recovery grants by the recipients, and the length of time needed to complete projects.

CONCLUDING OBSERVATIONS

In fiscal year 2013, the federal government obligated over $555 billion in grants for a wide array of activities. Effective oversight of internal controls is important for providing reasonable assurance to federal managers and taxpayers that grants are awarded properly, recipients are eligible, and federal grant funds are used as intended and in accordance with applicable laws and regulations.

Our review found that the five largest grant-making agencies' internal control assessment processes were consistent with the requirements in OMB Circular No. A-123 and its Appendix A. The findings from these assessment processes and from other reviews identified material weaknesses and significant deficiencies in grants management. OMB Circular No. A-123 notes that agency managers and staff should be encouraged to identify control deficiencies, as this reflects positively on the agency's commitment to recognizing and addressing management problems. Further, agencies are estimating that billions of dollars in improper payments occur each year in the grants programs.

Financial statement auditors, OIGs, and we continue to focus on grants internal controls through audits and reviews, and the agencies continue to use the results of these reviews and their own assessments to develop corrective actions and oversee internal controls of federal grants to ensure controls are in place and operating effectively.

AGENCY COMMENTS

We provided a draft of this report to the Secretaries of Health and Human Services, Education, Transportation, Agriculture, and Housing and Urban Development. In general, all five agencies concurred with the information in the report.

Education, DOT, USDA, and HUD also provided technical comments that were incorporated as appropriate. In addition, Education provided written comments. We also provided a draft of the report to the Director of OMB, and OMB responded that it had no comments.

Beryl H. Davis
Director,
Financial Management and Assurance

Appendix I: Objectives, Scope, and Methodology

Our objectives were to (1) examine whether the five largest grant-making agencies' internal control oversight processes for their grant programs were consistent with Office of Management and Budget (OMB) requirements and (2) describe internal control issues that have been reported related to the grants management process and key grant programs.[1]

Agency Selection

To select the agencies to include in our review and to obtain adequate coverage of federal grant dollars for fiscal year 2012—the most recently completed fiscal year at the time we started our review—we reviewed and summarized grant obligations data reported by agencies through USAspending.gov (as of November 19, 2012).[2] We decided to include the five agencies with the highest amounts of grants obligations, which accounted for almost 75 percent of total federal grant obligations for fiscal year 2012, excluding Medicaid, as discussed further below. The Departments of Health and Human Services (HHS), Education (Education), Transportation (DOT), Agriculture (USDA), and Housing and Urban Development (HUD) were the top five federal grant-making agencies based on grants obligations for fiscal year 2012. We also reviewed USAspending.gov data for fiscal year 2013 (as of January 27, 2014) and confirmed that the five largest grant-making agencies, based on obligations, in fiscal year 2012 remained the same in fiscal year 2013.

To assess the reliability of the USAspending.gov obligations data, we

1) reviewed recent GAO work that used the data and (2) compared results of ranking agencies by obligation amounts to the results of ranking agencies based on outlay amounts reported by OMB, as discussed below.3 In our recent work, we had assessed the reliability of USAspending.gov obligations data for a report we issued in September 2012 by (1) performing electronic testing of required data elements,
2) reviewing existing information about the data and the system that produced them, and (3) interviewing agency officials knowledgeable about the data, and we determined the data were sufficiently reliable for the purposes of that report. We also determined the data were sufficiently reliable for the purpose of selecting agencies and program offices to review for this report.

Further, to assess the reasonableness of our decision to use USAspending.gov obligations data to select the top five grant-making agencies, we reviewed OMB's Historical Table 12.3, Total Outlays for Grants to State and Local Governments, by Function, Agency and Program: 1940-2013, to determine the five largest grant-making agencies based on outlays for grants.[4]

We reviewed and summarized the data and found that the same five agencies we selected based on USAspending.gov data were also the top five grant-making agencies according to OMB's data. As the OMB budget data had undergone rigorous review by OMB, we considered them sufficiently reliable for the purposes of this report.[5]

In our review of the USAspending.gov data, we noted that grant obligations for Medicaid, one of HHS's grant programs, amounted to over 43 percent of total obligations incurred by the federal government for grants in fiscal year 2012.

We elected to exclude the Medicaid program from our review because it has been the subject of numerous reviews, including many by GAO and HHS's OIG, and by doing so, we were able to include HHS grant programs that otherwise would not have been covered in our review and still comply with our selection criteria to cover over 80 percent of each agency's grant obligations. (See table 5 and the related discussion.) Even after excluding Medicaid funds for fiscal year 2012, HHS was still the largest grant-making agency as measured by grant obligations.

During our initial planning work, we learned that agencies generally include cooperative agreements as part of their grants programs.[6] We also learned that although USAspending.gov data for Education categorize Pell Grants as "direct payments for a specified use" and do not identify them as "grants," Education considers Pell Grants to be grants, and the Pell Grant Program is Education's largest grant program.[7] Therefore, in addition to USAspending.gov's obligations for grants, we included in the scope of our review USAspending.gov amounts for cooperative agreements for the five agencies and Pell Grants. In addition, while HUD considers its Public Housing Operating Fund a subsidy program, and the *Catalog of Federal Domestic Assistance* categorizes the program as "direct payments for specified use," we included the program in our review based on the USAspending.gov categorization.[8]

In addition, during our planning work, we found that federal agencies rely on their program offices to provide assurance statements regarding the effectiveness of their internal controls. The program office assurance statements are then rolled up into the agency-wide management assurance statement, which the agencies are required by OMB to provide in their performance and accountability reports or agency financial reports.

Therefore, to obtain the most dollar coverage and cover the greatest subject area during our review, we selected the 2 or 3 largest program offices from each agency in order to cover over 80 percent of grant obligations for each agency, resulting in a total of 12 program offices, as shown in table 5. These 12 program offices together represented almost 75 percent of the total government-wide grants obligations (excluding Medicaid) for fiscal year 2012.

If we had not excluded Medicaid, the National Institutes of Health grant programs would not have been selected for inclusion in our review as the Centers for Medicare & Medicaid Services and the Administration for Children and Families together would have accounted for about 88 percent of HHS grant obligations. By excluding Medicaid, we were able to include the National Institutes of Health grant obligations, allowing us to cover additional grant programs.

Table 5. Amount and Percentage of Grant Obligations (Excluding Medicaid) for the Five Largest Grant-Making Agencies and Their Largest Program Offices, Fiscal Year 2012

Dollars in millions		
Agency and program offices	*Amount of grant obligations*	*Percentage of grant obligations*[a]
Department of Health and Human Services	*$98,400*	*100.0*
Administration for Children and Families	47,517	48.3
National Institutes of Health	22,242	22.6
Centers for Medicare and Medicaid Services[b]	10,569	10.7
Total percentage of obligations for selected program offices		*81.6*
Department of Education	*77,696*	*100.0*
Federal Student Aid	33,647	43.3
Office of Elementary and Secondary Education	21,859	28.1
Office of Special Education and Rehabilitative Services	15,840	20.4
Total percentage of obligations for selected program offices		*91.8*
Department of Transportation	*51,932*	*100.0*
Federal Highway Administration	34,454	66.3
Federal Transit Administration	11,871	22.9
Total percentage of obligations for selected program offices		*89.2*
Department of Agriculture	*30,876*	*100.0*
Food and Nutrition Service	28,296	91.6
National Institute of Food and Agriculture	1,238	4.0
Total percentage of obligations for selected program offices		*95.6*
Department of Housing and Urban Development	*12,107*	*100.0*
Office of Community Planning and Development	6,845	56.5
Office of Public and Indian Housing	5,131	42.4
Total percentage of obligations for selected program offices		
Total for agencies (excluding Medicaid)	$271,011	
Total for program offices (excluding Medicaid)	$239,509	

Source: GAO analysis of USAspending.gov data for fiscal year 2012 (as of November 19, 2012). | GAO-14-539.

[a]The program offices listed in this table are the two or three largest program offices in the agency, based on grant obligations. We selected those program offices that together constitute over 80 percent of an agency's grants obligations. Therefore, percentages for program offices in this table do not add up to 100 percent.

[b]The Centers for Medicare & Medicaid Services amounts exclude Medicaid obligations.

Examination of Agencies' Internal Control Oversight

To examine whether the five largest grant-making agencies' internal control oversight processes for their grants programs were consistent with OMB requirements, we focused on the agencies' fiscal year 2012 internal control evaluations performed to meet the internal control assessment and reporting requirements of OMB Circular No. A-123 and its Appendix A. We also considered *Standards for Internal Control in the Federal Government*, specifically, the standard for monitoring.[9] The standards provide the overall framework for establishing and maintaining internal control in federal programs. The monitoring standard states that internal control monitoring should assess the quality of performance over time and ensure that the findings of audits and other reviews are promptly resolved.

We obtained and analyzed documentation from the 12 program offices and from each of the five agencies' Office of the Chief Financial Officer. This documentation included or described relevant policies and procedures, risk assessments, testing methodologies and results, deficiencies found and corrective action plans developed and implemented as part of the fiscal year 2012 OMB Circular No. A-123 internal control assessment process. We used a data collection instrument to collect and summarize information obtained from the agencies. We did not reperform agency testing of internal controls or conduct our own testing of controls.

We also interviewed officials in the 12 program offices and officials from each of the five agencies' Office of the Chief Financial Officer and OIG about the agencies' assessment processes and oversight of grants- related internal control.

Identification of Reported Internal Control Issues

To identify internal control issues that have been reported related to the grants management process and key grant programs, we reviewed the agencies' financial statement audit reports for fiscal years 2012 and 2013 and relevant GAO and OIG reports issued in fiscal years 2012 and 2013 to identify grants-related internal control findings and recommendations. We also reviewed improper payment information reported by the five agencies in their agency financial reports for fiscal years 2012 and 2013 to determine whether the agencies identified improper payments in their grants programs.[10] We reviewed the OIGs' reports on their agencies' compliance with the criteria listed in the Improper Payments Elimination and Recovery Act of 2010 for fiscal years 2012 and 2013. We also reviewed management challenges reported by the agencies' OIGs for fiscal years 2012 and 2013.

We conducted this performance audit from November 2012 to July 2014 in accordance with generally accepted government auditing standards. Those standards require that we plan and perform the audit to obtain sufficient, appropriate evidence to provide a reasonable basis for our findings and conclusions based on our audit objectives. We believe that the evidence obtained provides a reasonable basis for our findings and conclusions based on our audit objectives.

End Notes

[1] As used in this report, "grant" refers to federal financial assistance that federal agencies provide to nonfederal entities for a public purpose pursuant to a grant agreement or a cooperative agreement and "grantee" refers to a nonfederal entity that enters into such agreements. Neither grant agreements nor cooperative agreements include an agreement under which is provided only direct U.S. government cash assistance to an individual, a subsidy; a loan, a loan guarantee, or insurance. Grant and cooperative agreements, however, are not identical. Under a grant agreement, the grantee is free to implement an agreed-upon program without substantial federal agency involvement. Under a cooperative agreement, the grantee has a significant amount of independence in carrying out its program, but the federal agency is involved in selected areas deemed essential to meeting program requirements and ensuring achievement of program objectives. These areas include, for example, approval of work plans, designation of key positions and approval of key personnel, and approval of monitoring and evaluation plans.

[2] The $555 billion represents the amount of obligations incurred for grants in fiscal year 2013 based on USAspending.gov data as of January 27, 2014. Established by the Office of Management and Budget pursuant to the Federal Funding Accountability and Transparency Act of 2006, Pub. L. No. 109-282, 120 Stat. 1186 (Sept. 26, 2006), USAspending.gov is a publicly available online database that allows users to search for detailed information about entities that are awarded federal grants, loans, contracts, and other forms of financial assistance. While the General Services Administration currently operates and maintains USAspending.gov, those responsibilities are being transferred to the Department of the Treasury's Bureau of the Fiscal Service. The transition is planned to be completed by September 30, 2014.

[3] We reviewed USAspending.gov data for fiscal year 2013 (as of January 27, 2014) and confirmed that these five agencies remained the largest grant-making agencies, based on obligations, in fiscal year 2013. See app. I for details.

[4] Federal grant obligations totaled over $564 billion in fiscal year 2012, according to USAspending.gov data as of November 19, 2012.

[5] An obligation is a definite commitment that creates a legal liability of the federal government for payment of goods and services ordered or received. A federal agency incurs an

obligation, for example, when it awards a grant. An outlay is a payment to liquidate a federal obligation.

[6] OMB collects data from federal agencies each year to prepare the President's budget. OMB uses these data for a number of purposes related to the budget, including producing the Historical Tables, which are publicly available on OMB's website. One series of Historical Tables contains information on federal outlays for grants to state and local governments. According to OMB, the purpose of this series of Historical Tables is to identify federal government outlays that constitute income to state and local governments to help finance their services.

[7] We also reviewed OMB data for fiscal year 2013 and confirmed that the five largest grant-making agencies, based on outlays, remained the same in fiscal year 2013.

[8] Office of Management and Budget, Management's Responsibility for Internal Control, OMB Circular No. A-123 (Dec. 21, 2004).

[9] GAO, Standards for Internal Control in the Federal Government, GAO/AIMD-00-21.3.1 (Washington, D.C.: November 1999).

[10] We selected for review programs categorized as grants in USAspending.gov. One of the programs selected, the Public Housing Operating Fund, is categorized in the Catalog of Federal Domestic Assistance (CFDA) as "direct payments for specified use," which is a form of financial assistance from the federal government provided directly to individuals, private firms, and other private institutions to encourage or subsidize a particular activity by conditioning the receipt of the assistance on a particular performance by the recipient. While not considered a grant program in the traditional sense by CFDA or by HUD, we included the program in our review based on the USAspending.gov categorization.

[11] The key provisions of the Federal Managers' Financial Integrity Act, Pub. L. No. 97-255, 96 Stat. 814 (Sept. 8, 1982), have been codified at 31 U.S.C. §3512 (c), (d).

[12] See the legislative history for Pub. L. No. 97-255, as reflected in 128 Cong. Rec. 19273- 19274 (Aug. 4, 1982) (statement of Senator Roth) and H. Rep. No. 97-38 (May 14, 1981).

[13] GAO/AIMD-00-21.3.1.

[14] OMB Circular No. A-123 provides that management categorize deficiencies identified during the annual internal control assessment as control deficiencies, reportable conditions, or material weaknesses. If management determines that a control deficiency, or a combination of deficiencies, could adversely affect the agency's ability to meet its objectives, management should categorize the deficiencies as reportable conditions, which are tracked and monitored within the agency. If management determines that the deficiencies are significant enough to report outside the agency, then they are to be considered material weaknesses and result in a qualified statement of assurance.

[15] The Single Audit Act, as amended and implemented, requires each reporting entity that expends the applicable threshold amount or more in federal awards, including grants and other assistance, in a fiscal year to obtain an annual "single audit," which includes an audit of the entity's financial statements and schedule of the expenditure of federal awards and a review of related internal controls. In December 2013, OMB issued new single audit guidance in Uniform Administrative Requirements, Cost Principles, and Audit Requirements for Federal Awards, which raised the single audit threshold amount from $500,000 to $750,000 effective for audits of nonfederal entity fiscal years beginning on or after December 26, 2014. See 78 Fed. Reg. 78590 (Dec. 26, 2013).

[16] Under the Improper Payments Information Act of 2002, as amended, improper payments are statutorily defined as any payment that should not have been made or that was made in an incorrect amount under statutory, contractual, administrative, or other legally applicable

requirements. Incorrect amounts are overpayments or underpayments that are made to eligible recipients (including inappropriate denials of payment or service, any payment that does not account for credit for applicable discounts, payments that are for the incorrect amount, and duplicate payments). An improper payment also includes any payment that was made to an ineligible recipient or for an ineligible good or service, or payments for goods or services not received (except for such payments authorized by law). In addition, pursuant to OMB implementing guidance, when an agency's review is unable to discern whether a payment was proper as a result of insufficient documentation or lack of documentation, this payment must also be considered an improper payment.

[17] Pub. L. No. 107-300, 116 Stat. 2350 (Nov. 26, 2002). 18Pub. L. No. 111-204, 124 Stat. 2224 (July 22, 2010).

[19] We did not consider this statute (Pub. L. No. 112-248) in this report because it was not in effect in fiscal year 2012, the time period covered by our review.

[20] Section 2(g)(1) of IPERA required the Director of OMB to prescribe guidance for agencies to implement the requirements of IPERA.

[21] Office of Management and Budget, Issuance of Revised Parts I and II to Appendix C of OMB Circular A-123, OMB Memorandum M-11-16 (Washington, D.C.: Apr. 14, 2011), and Issuance of Part III to OMB Circular A-123, Appendix C, OMB Memorandum M-10-13 (Washington, D.C.: Mar. 22, 2010).

[22] Beginning in fiscal year 2014, IPERA reduced the threshold for "significant" improper payment from 2.5 percent to 1.5 percent. Also, pursuant to the Disaster Relief Appropriations Act, 2013, Pub. L. No. 113-2, § 904(b), 127 Stat. 4, 17 (Jan. 29, 2013), agencies will be required to estimate improper payments in programs funded by Hurricane Sandy relief funds.

[23] The agencies also selected other processes and programs to evaluate controls in fiscal year 2012. The scope of our review is focused on the portions of the OMB Circular No. A123 process that evaluated grants-related controls.

[24] GAO/AIMD-00-21.3.1, 20.

[25] Management will give a qualified statement of assurance when there are material weaknesses to report and will give an unqualified statement of assurance when no material weaknesses are being reported.

[26] Undisbursed balances or unliquidated obligations are funds that the federal awarding agency has obligated by entering into a grant agreement but that the grantee has not drawn down or the federal awarding agency has not disbursed.

[27] A deficiency in internal control exists when the design or operation of a control does not allow management or employees, in the normal course of performing their assigned functions, to prevent, or detect and correct misstatements on a timely basis. Financial statement auditors, who are independent of management, categorize internal control deficiencies as material weaknesses or significant deficiencies. For financial audit purposes, a material weakness is a deficiency, or a combination of deficiencies, in internal control such that there is a reasonable possibility that a material misstatement of the entity's financial statements will not be prevented, or detected and corrected, on a timely basis. A significant deficiency is a deficiency, or a combination of deficiencies, in internal control that is less severe than a material weakness yet important enough to merit attention by those charged with governance. The definitions and reporting requirements for control deficiencies identified in financial statement audits differ from those used under OMB Circular No. A-123.

[28] GAO, Grants Management: Action Needed to Improve the Timeliness of Grant Closeouts by Federal Agencies, GAO-12-360 (Washington, D.C.: Apr. 16, 2012).

[29] The Forest Service accounted for about 1 percent of USDA's grant obligations in fiscal year 2012 and was not included in our review.

[30] FFMIA requires the departments and agencies covered by the Chief Financial Officers Act of 1990 (CFO Act agencies) to implement and maintain financial management systems that comply substantially with federal financial management systems requirements, applicable federal accounting standards, and the U.S. Government Standard General Ledger at the transaction level. FFMIA defines the term financial management systems to include the financial systems and the financial portions of mixed systems necessary to support financial management, including automated and manual processes, procedures, controls, data, hardware, software, and support personnel dedicated to the operation and maintenance of system functions. See Federal Financial Management Improvement Act of 1996, Pub. L. No. 104-208, div. A., § 101(f), title VIII, 110 Stat. 3009, 3009-389 (Sept. 30, 1996) (reprinted in 31 U.S.C. § 3512 note).

[31] GAO, Financial Audit: U.S. Government's Fiscal Years 2013 and 2012 Consolidated Financial Statements, GAO-14-319R (Washington, D.C.: Feb. 27, 2014), and Financial Audit: U.S. Government's Fiscal Years 2012 and 2011 Consolidated Financial Statements, GAO-13-271R (Washington, D.C.: Jan. 17, 2013).

[32] GAO, Temporary Assistance for Needy Families: More Accountability Needed to Reflect Breadth of Block Grant Services, GAO-13-33 (Washington, D.C.: Dec. 6, 2012).

[33] Pub. L. No. 111-5, 123 Stat. 115 (Feb. 17, 2009).

[34] GAO, Race to the Top: Reform Efforts Are Under Way and Information Sharing Could Be Improved, GAO-11-658 (Washington, D.C.: June 30, 2011).

[35] Department of Health and Human Services Office of Inspector General, NIH Administration of the Clinical and Translational Science Awards Program, OEI-07-09-00300 (Washington, D.C.: December 2011).

[36] Department of Transportation Office of Inspector General, Improvements Needed in FTA's Grant Oversight Program, MH-2012-168 (Washington, D.C.: Aug. 2, 2012).

[37] Department of Agriculture Office of Inspector General, American Recovery and Reinvestment Act of 2009, National School Lunch Program Equipment Assistance Grants, Report 27703-0001-HQ (Washington, D.C.: Feb. 15, 2012).

[38] Department of Housing and Development Office of Inspector General, Controls Over the Timeliness of CDBG Entitlement Spending, 2013-NY-0003 (Washington, D.C.: July 19, 2013).

[39] HUD did not report estimated improper payments for its grant programs. According to the OIG's April 2014 report on HUD's compliance with IPERA, HUD had previously identified Community Development Block Grant programs as susceptible to improper payments; however, HUD found that estimated improper payments in those programs were below the $10 million threshold for 2 consecutive years. Therefore, in 2007, OMB approved HUD's request for relief from the annual improper payment reporting for the Community Development Block Grant programs. In its fiscal year 2013 agency financial report, HUD noted that it will continue to conduct an annual risk assessment of the programs and provide results annually to OMB.

[40] Department of Health and Human Services Office of Inspector General, U.S. Department of Health and Human Services Met Many Requirements of the Improper Payments Information Act of 2002 But Was Not Fully Compliant, A-17-13-52000 (Washington, D.C.: March 2013), and U.S. Department of Health and Human Services Met Many Requirements of the Improper Payments Information Act of 2002 But Did Not Fully Comply for Fiscal Year 2013, A-17-14-52000 (Washington, D.C.: April 2014).

[41] Department of Agriculture Office of Inspector General, U.S. Department of Agriculture Improper Payments Elimination and Recovery Act of 2010 Compliance Review for Fiscal Year 2012, 50024-0004-11 (Washington, D.C.: Mar. 14, 2013), and U.S. Department of Agriculture Improper Payments Elimination and Recovery Act of 2010 Compliance Review for Fiscal Year 2013, 50024-0005-11 (Washington, D.C.: Apr. 15, 2014).

[42] According to the Food and Nutrition Service, the study will develop and validate models for updating erroneous payment estimates, among other things. The Food and Nutrition Service expects the final report on the study in early 2015.

[43] Department of Education Office of Inspector General, U.S. Department of Education's Compliance with the Improper Payments Elimination and Recovery Act of 2010 for Fiscal Year 2012, ED-OIG/A03N0001 (Washington, D.C.: Mar. 15, 2013), and U.S. Department of Education's Compliance with the Improper Payments Elimination and Recovery Act of 2010 for Fiscal Year 2013, ED-OIG/A19O0002 (Washington, D.C.: Apr. 15, 2014).

[44] Department of Transportation Office of Inspector General, DOT's FY 2012 Improper Payment Reporting Generally Complies with IPERA, FI-2013-053 (Washington, D.C.: Mar. 14, 2013), and Accuracy and Reliability of DOT's Improper Payment Reporting Can Be Improved, FI-2014-037 (Washington, D.C.: April 15, 2014).

[45] Pub. L. No. 106-531, 114 Stat. 2537 (Nov. 22, 2000), codified, as amended, at 31 U.S.C. § 3516.

End Notes for Appenix I

[1] As used in this report, "grant" refers to federal financial assistance that federal agencies provide to nonfederal entities for a public purpose pursuant to a grant agreement or a cooperative agreement and "grantee" refers to a nonfederal entity that enters into such agreements. Neither grant agreements nor cooperative agreements include an agreement under which is provided only direct U.S. government cash assistance to an individual, a subsidy, a loan, a loan guarantee, or insurance. Grant and cooperative agreements, however, are not identical. Under a grant agreement, the grantee is free to implement an agreed-upon program without substantial federal agency involvement. Under a cooperative agreement, the grantee has a significant amount of independence in carrying out its program, but the federal agency is involved in selected areas deemed essential to meeting program requirements and ensuring achievement of program objectives. These areas include, for example, approval of work plans, designation of key positions and approval of key personnel, and approval of monitoring and evaluation plans.

[2] Established by OMB pursuant to the Federal Funding Accountability and Transparency Act of 2006, Pub. L. No. 109-282, 120 Stat. 1186 (Sept. 26, 2006), USAspending.gov is a publicly available online database that allows users to search for detailed information about entities that are awarded federal grants, loans, contracts, and other forms of financial assistance. While the General Services Administration operates and maintains USAspending.gov, those responsibilities are being transferred to the Department of the Treasury's Bureau of the Fiscal Service. The transition is planned to be completed by September 30, 2014.

[3] An obligation is a definite commitment that creates a legal liability of the federal government for payment of goods and services ordered or received. A federal agency incurs an obligation, for example, when it awards a grant. An outlay is a payment to liquidate a federal obligation.

[4] OMB collects data from federal agencies each year to prepare the President's budget. OMB uses these data for a number of purposes related to the budget, including producing the Historical Tables, which are publicly available on OMB's website. One series of Historical Tables contains information on federal outlays for grants to state and local governments. According to OMB, the purpose of this series of Historical Tables is to identify federal government outlays that constitute income to state and local governments to help finance their services.

[5] We also reviewed OMB data for fiscal year 2013 and confirmed that the five largest grant-making agencies, based on outlays, remained the same in fiscal year 2013.

[6] Like grants, cooperative agreements are a form of financial assistance. The distinguishing factor between a grant and a cooperative agreement is that cooperative agreements require a greater degree of federal participation or involvement during the performance of the work activities.

[7] "Direct payments for a specific use" is another form of financial assistance whereby the federal government directly provides payments to individuals, private firms, and other private institutions to encourage or to subsidize a particular activity by conditioning the receipt of the assistance on a specific action by the recipient.

[8] As we reported in our September 2012 report Grants to State and Local Governments: An Overview of Federal Funding Levels and Selected Challenges, GAO-12-1016, determining a definitive number of federal grant programs presents certain difficulties. The Catalog of Federal Domestic Assistance (CFDA) is the single authoritative, government-wide compendium and source document for descriptions of federal programs that provide assistance or benefits to the public. Officials from the General Services Administration told us that each agency determines how to organize and describe its programs for publication in the CFDA, as long as the agency adheres to the underlying requirement to describe the program's legal authority, administering office, funding, purpose, benefits, and beneficiaries.

[9] GAO, Standards for Internal Control in the Federal Government, GAO/AIMD-00-21.3.1 (Washington, D.C.: November 1999).

[10] The amounts and error rates the agencies reported for improper payments are based on the amounts of program outlays, which differ from the obligation amounts we used to select the agencies. The differences could be related to timing differences, as obligations are recorded when grants are awarded, and outlays are recorded when funds are actually disbursed to grantees. Also, the sources for the amounts differ. We used obligations data reported to USAspending.gov (as of November 19, 2012), and the outlay data the agencies reported came from other agency sources of expenditure data.

In: Federal Grant Management and Controls ISBN: 978-1-63482-559-7
Editor: Dana T. Greer

Chapter 2

GRANTS MANAGEMENT: PROGRAMS AT HHS AND HUD COLLECT ADMINISTRATIVE COST INFORMATION BUT DIFFERENCES IN COST CAPS AND DEFINITIONS CREATE CHALLENGES*

United States Government Accountability Office

ABBREVIATIONS

AITR	Allergy, Immunology and Transplantation Research
CCDF	Child Care and Development Fund
CDBG	Community Development Block Grant
HHS	Department of Health and Human Services
HOME	HOME Investment Partnerships Program
HUD	Department of Housing and Urban Development
MHSC	Multifamily Housing Service Coordinators
NIH	National Institutes of Health
OMB	Office of Management and Budget

* This is an edited, reformatted and augmented version of The United States Government Accountability Office publication, GAO-15-118, dated December 2014.

WHY GAO DID THIS STUDY

The federal government spends billions of dollars on various grants to achieve diverse purposes. The total cost of a grant includes both program costs that directly support the grant's mission and services and administrative costs to run the program. These administrative activities, such as managing finances, are essential. It is important for agencies to track the cost of these activities to provide accountability for efficient use of federal resources.

GAO was asked to review how costs associated with the administration of grants are tracked and the availability of this information. GAO examined (1) the extent to which selected federal agencies and grantees have mechanisms and guidance in place to distinguish between administrative and program costs and to facilitate the availability of these data to Congress and the public; and (2) the extent to which there are challenges that hinder the comparability of grant administrative cost data. For this review GAO selected six grant programs—three in HHS and three in the Department of Housing and Urban Development (HUD). Agencies and grant programs were selected in part based on obligation amounts and grant types. GAO reviewed each program's statutes, regulations, guidance, and grant documents, as applicable, and interviewed agency officials. Although GAO's findings are not generalizable, they are indicative of the wide variation associated with the mechanisms and guidance for tracking grant administrative costs.

GAO received and incorporated, as appropriate, technical comments from HHS. HUD did not provide comments.

WHAT GAO FOUND

All six of the grant programs GAO reviewed had mechanisms in place to capture the administrative costs charged to their grant programs, either via a computerized system or paper reporting. All the programs reported that they reviewed their grantees' costs for appropriateness. Two of the programs make administrative cost data available online. The programs GAO reviewed track administrative costs in different ways. For some programs administrative and program costs are reported separately, while for others they are included in the same line items. Administrative costs reported to the federal government may understate the actual cost to administer a grant program. GAO found examples of grantees absorbing part of the costs to administer a grant. Some primary grant recipients stated that when such costs were not reimbursed by the federal grant, they would cover those expenses themselves. Another grantee said he relies on state appropriations to cover the majority of administrative costs.

GAO identified two factors that hinder the comparability of administrative cost data in the programs it reviewed. First, is the existence of cost caps. These caps limit the amount of the grant that may be charged as administrative costs, and thereby affect what is reported to the federal government as administrative costs. For the programs GAO reviewed caps ranged from 5 to 26 percent, with one program having no cap. This variation can make some programs look more administratively expensive than others. Second, differences in what is defined as an administrative cost can present an even greater challenge to comparing costs across programs. Programs have different missions, priorities, services, and clients; as a result definitions of administrative costs vary from program to program. Therefore, different programs may treat similar costs differently. A cost that may be classified as administrative in one program may be considered a direct program delivery cost by another. For example, the salary of an employee who enrolls participants in one Department of Health and Human Services (HHS) program is considered a program cost but an employee who holds a similar position determining the eligibility of participants in another HHS program may be considered an administrative cost depending on the state where it is administered. This variation in definitions means that a program with high administrative costs may not be less efficient than a program with low administrative costs.

Given these issues, it is challenging to collect comparable information for different grant programs. Any use of information on administrative costs needs to recognize these concerns particularly when comparing programs with different types of objectives, projects, or services. Comparisons of costs may be appropriate when reviewing programs that fulfill similar missions or provide similar services. However, comparisons across different types of grant programs should be made with caution.

* * *

December 12, 2014
Congressional Requesters:

The federal government provides grants to a wide range of recipients—including state and local governments, for-profit and nonprofit entities, and public and private universities—to achieve national objectives. The government spends a substantial amount of money on these grants. According to the Office of Management and Budget (OMB), state and local governments alone received about $546 billion in federal grants in fiscal year 2013.[1] The total cost of a grant includes two components: (1) program costs that directly support the grant's mission and services; and (2) administrative costs, such as payroll and clerical support, to run the grant program. It is important for agencies that administer grants to track these costs—including the portion spent to reimburse grantees for their administrative costs—because such tracking allows the agencies to provide accountability for efficient use of resources. Further, tracking these costs helps agencies assess the changes in the balance between grant administrative costs and program costs. However, as budgets grow more constrained, this drive for efficiency can create a tension between a program's capacity to deliver services and the actual administrative costs of doing so.

The recently enacted Digital Accountability and Transparency Act of 2014 (DATA Act) is intended to increase accountability and transparency of federal spending and establish government-wide financial data standards.[2] Towards this end, OMB and the Department of the Treasury (Treasury) are developing these standards, which could include administrative spending.[3] In addition, legislation has been introduced in Congress that could also affect how agencies publicly report on program administrative costs.[4] As agencies implement the DATA Act and as Congress examines whether to require additional reporting on administrative costs, it is important to consider what these costs represent, how they are calculated, and the challenges in making comparisons across different programs.

You asked us to review how costs associated with the administration of grants are tracked and the availability of this information. This report examines (1) the extent to which selected federal agencies and grantees have mechanisms and guidance in place to distinguish between administrative and program costs and to facilitate the availability of these data to Congress and the public; and (2) the extent to which there are challenges that hinder the comparability of grant administrative cost data. To address these objectives, we selected two agencies for this review— the Departments of Health and Human Services (HHS) and Housing and Urban Development (HUD). We selected HHS because it manages the largest share of federal grants in terms of both obligation amount and number of grant programs. We included HUD to obtain management perspectives on a different set of programs and issues. We then selected three grant programs at each of these agencies with the aim of identifying both higher-dollar value grants relative to other agency programs as well as a variety of types of grants (project and formula) and grantees (state and local governments, nonprofit organizations, and for-profit entities).

At HHS we selected the following grant programs:

- Child Care and Development Fund (CCDF);
- Head Start; and
- Allergy, Immunology and Transplantation Research (AITR).

At HUD we selected the following grant programs:

- HOME Investment Partnerships Program (HOME);
- Community Development Block Grant (CDBG); and
- Multifamily Housing Service Coordinators (MHSC).

See table 1 in the background for information on each of these programs.

To determine the extent to which selected federal agencies and grantees have mechanisms and guidance in place to distinguish between administrative and program costs, we reviewed regulations, program guidance, grant documents, and statutes as applicable for each program. Additionally, we interviewed agency officials responsible for each of the selected grant programs to understand how these programs collect administrative cost data; the guidance, training, and technical assistance they provide grantees; and their requirements and experiences with determining and reporting administrative costs. To inform our work on government-wide efforts to collect grant administrative cost information, we interviewed staff at OMB's Office of Federal Financial Management.

To examine the extent to which there are challenges that hinder the comparability of grant administrative cost data we used OMB data on federal grants to select states with varying amounts of federal grant obligations.[5] We selected Massachusetts and New Hampshire as states receiving higher and lower amounts of federal grant dollars, respectively. We then selected primary grant recipients within those states with the highest grant obligation for each selected grant program in that state. To better understand grant administrative costs, grant management, and cost principles we reviewed our previous reports on these topics as well as those by the Congressional Research Service and the Congressional Budget Office.[6] See appendix I for more details on program selection and our overall objectives, scope, and methodology.

BACKGROUND

We conducted this performance audit from January 2014 to December 2014 in accordance with generally accepted government auditing standards. Those standards require that we plan and perform the audit to obtain sufficient, appropriate evidence to provide a reasonable basis for our findings and conclusions based on our audit objectives. We believe that the evidence obtained provides a reasonable basis for our findings and conclusions based on our audit objectives.

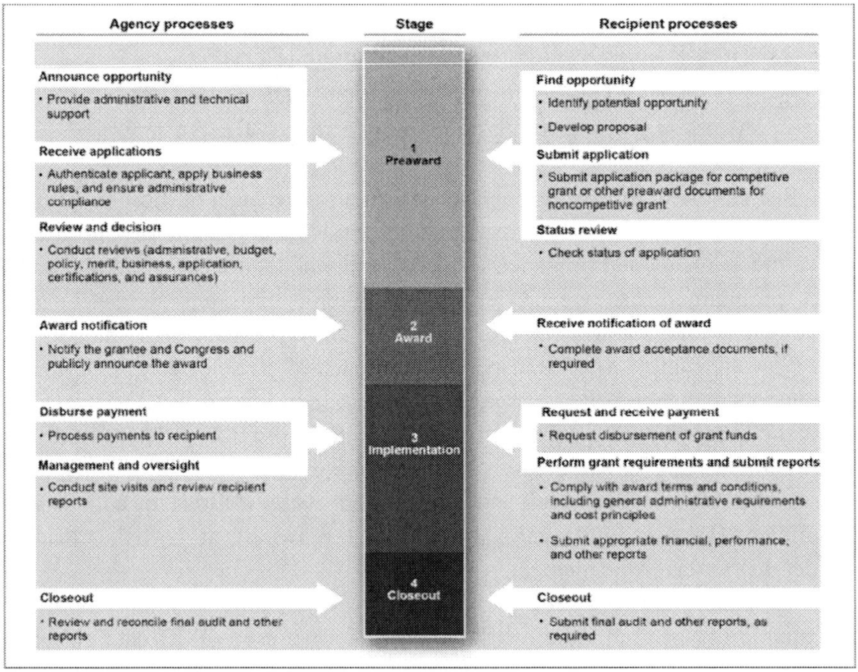

Source: GAO. | GAO-15-118.

Figure 1. Grant Life Cycle for Federal Grant-Making Agencies and Grant Recipients.

The federal government provides grants to a variety of recipients as a form of financial assistance to accomplish a particular public purpose authorized by law. Grant recipients include for-profit and nonprofit entities; public and private universities; and state, local, and tribal governments. Some grant programs also permit the granting of funds from primary grant recipient to subawardees. While there is substantial variation among grant types, competitively awarded federal grants generally follow a life cycle comprising various stages—pre-award (announcement and application), award, implementation, and closeout—as shown in figure 1.

Grant programs are established through legislation that may specify particular objectives, eligibility requirements, and other conditions, and grant-making agencies may impose additional requirements on recipients. Additionally, grant programs are typically subject to a wide range of accountability requirements under their authorizing or appropriations statutes and implementing regulations. Congress may also impose increased reporting and oversight requirements at the agency or recipient level. Grant-making agencies and their programs are also subject to crosscutting requirements applicable to most assistance programs.

Administrative Costs

Administrative activities such as managing finances and facilities, ensuring quality, and reporting project status are essential to the operation of grant programs. These administrative costs may be charged directly or indirectly to a grant depending on individual program guidelines and whether the grantee has an approved indirect rate agreement.[7] A *direct cost* is one that can be specifically identified with the individual grant objective and is charged to that specific grant. Direct costs include, for example, a researcher's salary and equipment. *Indirect costs* represent a grantee's general support expenses that cannot be specifically identified with an individual grant project. Indirect costs include, for example, building utilities and administrative staff salaries (see figure 2). To determine the proportion of indirect costs that may be charged to federally funded awards, grantees use a mechanism called the *indirect cost rate.* The procedure for requesting an indirect cost rate varies based on the type of grantee organization. In the case of higher educational institutions, the rate is established based on a historical fiscal year of cost data from a school and is applied to each of its individual research awards.[8]

As we have previously reported, there is no government-wide definition of what constitutes an administrative cost.[9] Programs have different missions, priorities, services, and clients, and jurisdiction for the programs are spread among numerous congressional committees; therefore federal agencies' definitions of allowable (or prohibited) administrative costs vary from program to program.

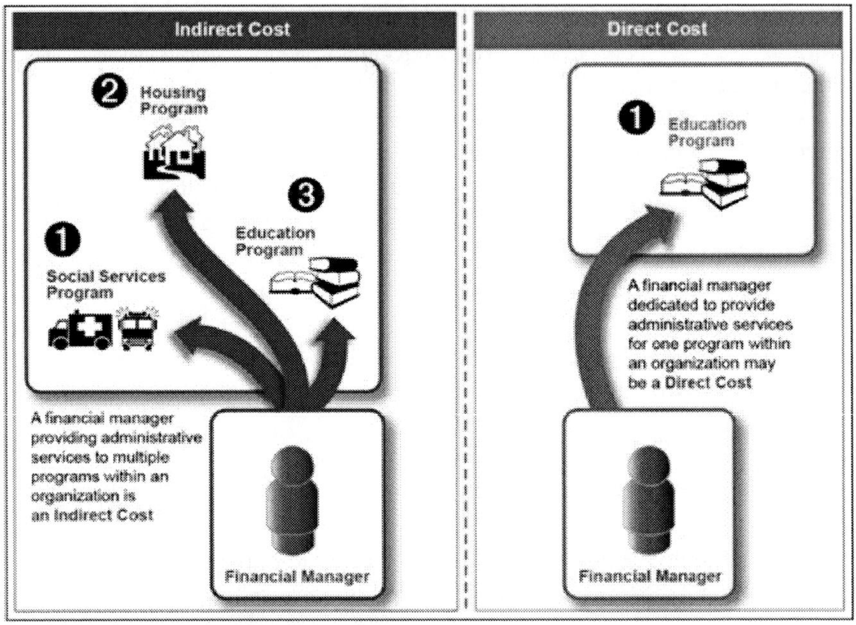

Source: GAO analysis of CMB Circular No. A-21 | GAO-15-118.

Figure 2. Two Options for Charging Administrative Costs under OMB Guidance on Cost Principles.

We have also previously concluded that funding gaps for grant indirect costs which, depending on the program, may represent a large portion of administrative costs, may compromise the nonprofit sector's ability to partner with the federal government to provide services and may ultimately risk the viability of the sector.[10] In a 2013 study, the Urban Institute found that limits on administrative costs are concerning for nonprofits because they must find other ways to cover these expenses. This study also stated that trying to minimize overhead costs could lead nonprofits to offer low pay for administrative positions, which could make it difficult to recruit and retain skilled and experienced staff.[11]

Guidance on Cost Principles

OMB is responsible for developing government-wide guidance to ensure that grants are managed properly and that grant funds are spent in accordance with applicable laws and regulations.[12] OMB provides guidance on administrative requirements, cost principles, and audit requirements for federal awards. Until recently, OMB guidance came in the form of circulars for specific grants management areas to different types of grantees. For example, OMB Circular No. A-21 provided the principles for determining the types of direct and indirect costs that may be claimed and the methods for allocating such costs to federally funded projects at educational institutions. OMB had similar guidance on cost principles for state and local governments, Indian tribal governments, and nonprofit organizations. In December 2013, OMB consolidated its grants management circulars into a single document, *Uniform Administrative Requirements, Cost Principles, and Audit Requirements for Federal Awards* (Uniform Guidance), to streamline its guidance, promote consistency among grantees, and reduce administrative burden on nonfederal entities.[13] OMB staff told us that although the new Uniform Guidance is intended to create a framework for the allocation of grant costs, decisions about how these costs are allocated are made at the award level.[14] The new Uniform Guidance is scheduled to go into effect for grantees on December 26, 2014, and officials at both HHS and HUD told us they were evaluating the changes and its effects on their programs and regulations.

Selected Agencies and Programs

To provide examples for this review, we selected six grant programs at two federal grant-making agencies (see table 1). These programs are managed by a variety of subagencies and reflect different program objectives.

Agencies Reviewed Have Mechanisms in Place to Collect Data on Federal Grant Administrative Costs, but These Data May Not Reflect Actual Cost of Administration

Although grant-making agencies are not required to track grant administrative cost data specifically, all six of the grant programs we reviewed collect grant administrative cost data in some form. Each of the grant programs we reviewed had mechanisms in place to capture the administrative costs charged to their grant programs, via either a computerized system or paper reporting.[15] However, each program's data collection system varied, as follows:

- HHS's On-Line Data Collection System used for the CCDF grant and HUD's Integrated Disbursement & Information System used for both HOME and CDBG are computerized data collection systems available to the grantee and agency that capture grant program budgetary information and actual post-award expenditure reporting.
- The Head Start Enterprise System collects grant budget estimates electronically during the program's grant application process.

Table I. Selected Grant Programs

Program name	Agency/sub-agency	Objectives
HOME Investment Partnerships Program	HUD/Community Planning and Development	To expand the supply of affordable housing, particularly rental housing, for low and very low income Americans.
Community Development Block Grant (CDBG) program for Entitlement Communities	HUD/Community Planning and Development	To develop viable urban communities by providing decent housing, a suitable living environment, and expanding economic opportunities, principally for persons of low and moderate income.
Multifamily Housing Service Coordinators	HUD/Office of Housing	To link elderly, especially frail and disabled, or disabled nonelderly assisted housing and neighborhood residents to supportive services in thegeneral community.
Child Care and Development Fund (CCDF)	HHS/Administration for Children and Families	To promote family economic self-sufficiency and to help children succeed in school and life through affordable, high-quality early care and afterschool programs.
Head Start	HHS/Administration for Children and Families	To promote school readiness by enhancing the social and cognitive development of low-income children.

Program name	Agency/sub-agency	Objectives
Allergy, Immunology and Transplantation Research (AITR)	HHS/National Institutes of Health	To assist public and private nonprofit institutions and individuals to establish, expand, and improve biomedical research and research trainingin allergic and immunologic diseases and related areas to assist public, private, and commercial institutions to conduct developmental research.

Source: GAO analysis of CFDA and HHS program descriptions. | GAO-15-118.

Reporting of actual expenses incurred is captured in paper form at the regional office level.

- The Multifamily Housing Service Coordinators program uses the Line of Credit Control System to disburse and track payment of grant funds. The system may be accessed through a voice-response system or a computerized system. In addition to these systems, documentation is provided in paper form to the regional office where the grant is managed.
- Electronic Research Administration Commons is a web-based interface where National Institutes of Health (NIH) grantees share administrative information about grants. It also collects AITR grantees' Federal Financial Reports.

Officials for all of the selected programs reported that they use these systems to review their grantees' costs for appropriateness. Such reviews also help to ensure that the data collected are accurate if they are used for evaluating the programs' effectiveness. With the exception of the AITR program, which is managed at headquarters, all of the programs we reviewed performed compliance checks on fiscal reporting at the regional office level where the grants are managed. For five of the six programs in our review, officials said their analysis of administrative costs was focused on ensuring compliance with the grants' administrative cost caps and approved indirect rate agreements. Agency officials also told us that when a grantee's total federal expenditures exceed an audit threshold, all six programs rely on the single audit process to identify deficiencies in grantee accounting, internal controls, and financial management.[16] Two of the six programs we reviewed—

CDBG and CCDF—make their grant administrative cost data available to the public via their websites.

The six programs we reviewed track grant expenses in different ways, which can make it challenging to identify aggregate administrative costs. For some of these programs, administrative costs and program costs may be included in the same line items and program officials told us that separating these costs would be labor intensive. For example, program officials explained that for the AITR program they do not specifically track grant administrative costs. Instead, grant program costs are reported as either direct or indirect costs because recipients are required to use the *Federal Financial Report* to report on grant expenditures and that report captures indirect costs.[17] NIH officials explained that administrative costs are normally charged as indirect costs but if the administrative services are integral to a major project and the administrative costs can be specifically attributed to the project, they may be charged as direct costs to the grant.[18] Therefore, interpreting indirect costs as administrative costs could miss administrative costs charged as direct costs to the grant.

Further complicating this issue, NIH officials explained that primary grant recipients report their subgrantee's direct and indirect expenses under the primary recipient's total costs on the *Federal Financial Report.* There is no requirement to specifically track grant administrative cost data for a grant's subgrantee and the current federal financial reporting mechanism for the AITR grant does not facilitate identifying all administrative costs. According to NIH officials, identifying administrative costs reported under the total cost line item would be onerous under the current financial information collection method since this would entail additional auditing at both the primary grantee and subgrantee levels. Additionally, consistent with OMB guidance, indirect cost rates are to be based on historical costs incurred by an institution and applied to all grants received by that institution for a set period. While using such a rate may prove efficient for reporting purposes, these rates are a blunt instrument by which to determine actual administrative costs for any one grant program.

For the grant programs we reviewed, financial reporting systems varied in their ability to aggregate program-wide administrative cost information. HUD's Integrated Disbursement & Information System—a nationwide database that provides HUD with current information on CDBG and HOME program activities—includes grant administrative cost information. In contrast, the Head Start program does not currently have a system in place that allows it to aggregate grant administrative cost information across grantees.

Instead, Head Start grantees report their expenses after they are incurred on a SF-425 paper form retained at the regional office level. HHS officials are planning to collect the SF-425 electronically on the GrantSolutions platform beginning in late 2015 and should be able to display these data electronically in the Head Start Enterprise System. According to HHS officials, the new method of data collection and management should enable Head Start staff to aggregate actual expenditure data—categorized as programmatic or administrative costs— for analysis and reporting at the headquarters level, which would potentially facilitate reporting these costs. This mechanism should facilitate program-wide aggregation of administrative costs and is a necessary first step to obtain an overall understanding of a program's administrative costs.

Just as the mechanisms to collect information differ across the grant programs we reviewed, there is also variation in guidance and training regarding the reporting of grant administrative costs. The six programs we reviewed provide some form of written guidance or instruction regarding the allocation of administrative and program costs. Head Start provides program-specific resources, written guides, and interactive training modules on its website—the Early Childhood Learning and Knowledge Center. The AITR, CCDF, CDBG, and HOME programs also provide resources and guidance online.[19] Applicable administrative cost definitions for MHSC are not included in the management handbook for the grant program. However, officials explained that a list of allowable administrative costs does exist in the grant's Notice of Funding Availability. With regard to training, program officials with Head Start, CDBG, HOME, and CCDF told us they provide grantees across the country with training on a wide variety of program-specific and fiscal management issues. For example, HUD officials explained that they offer training on identifying allowable administrative costs and that they plan to provide training in financial management via interactive modules online.

NIH officials told us they provide written guidance and offer special training upon request, but NIH does not provide training to all of its grantees for the AITR grant program. NIH officials said that grantees tend to hire external consultants to assist them with preparing indirect cost rate proposals. MHSC officials said that they do not provide centralized training on administrative costs to grantees, but training is provided by some field offices that determine a need for such training. In addition to written guidance on fiscal information, all six of the programs we reviewed described processes for providing technical support to grantees on request.

Grant recipients of all the programs we reviewed told us that since administrative costs are not always reimbursed by their federal grants they must cover some administrative expenses themselves. The Urban Institute made the same point in a survey of nonprofits that receive government grants.[20] This review found that half of survey respondents said their government grants and contracts expressly excluded or limited reimbursements for their program and organizational administrative costs.

Unreimbursed administrative costs in the programs we reviewed ranged from costs related to the grant managers who oversaw the grant program to costs that covered centralized business services such as accounting or human resources. Functions like these support the administration of the grant but are not directly related to its aims or purposes. We found examples of grantees absorbing part of the costs to administer a grant. An official at a state department of health receiving a CCDF grant explained that she analyzes administrative costs and when her organization approaches its federal cost cap she pays these expenses from the state's general fund. Another CCDF state grantee told us that he relies on state appropriations to cover the majority of administrative costs, and therefore his organization's federally reported administrative costs remain well under the cap set by the program. Since state funds were available to cover a portion of the administrative expenses, he explained that the organization did not have to claim from the federal government all the administrative expenses to which they were entitled. To the extent that only administrative costs charged to the grant are reported, these reports may understate the actual administrative costs.

The actual cost to administer a grant may also be affected by whether oversight responsibilities are extended over long periods, as is required by some federal grant programs. If a grantee has oversight responsibilities for an ongoing portfolio of work it may incur greater administrative costs than a grantee with a shorter-term project with defined beginning and end dates. For example, primary grant recipients of the HOME program are required to oversee HOME-funded rental properties for up to 20 years after construction. According to a HOME grantee, as the portfolio of properties grows the HOME oversight requirements cause the grantee's oversight costs to increase year after year. However, the HOME grant administrative cost cap does not increase to cover these increased oversight costs associated with a grantee's growing portfolio of properties over time. Because of this, a HOME grantee told us that as these costs increase over time she will need to absorb these costs, covering them with resources from both HOME administrative funds and state funds. In some cases, the grantee has reviewed HOME grant amounts and actual HOME administrative costs and chosen to allocate funds to fewer units and to fewer projects because of the oversight costs that will be incurred over time.

VARIATIONS IN ADMINISTRATIVE COST CAPS AND DEFINITIONS HINDER MEANINGFUL COMPARISONS OF GRANT ADMINISTRATIVE COST DATA ACROSS PROGRAMS

Two challenges to comparing administrative costs across grant programs are the variation in cost caps and differences in administrative cost definitions. These two issues are different, but they intersect. The variation in administrative cost caps—the limit to the amount of the grant that may be charged as administrative costs to the federal government— presents challenges to comparing costs across programs. Of the six grant programs we reviewed, administrative cost caps ranged from 5 percent for CCDF to a 26 percent administrative cost cap for education institutions receiving AITR grants.[21] The Multifamily Housing Service Coordinators grant program has no cap.[22] As a result of this variation, the administrative costs of some programs may appear more expensive than others. For example, CDBG's 20 percent cost cap could result in higher administrative charges to the grant than the CCDF's 5 percent cost cap. According to HUD data, CDBG administrative and planning expenses in fiscal year 2012 were approximately 16 percent and, according to HHS data, CCDF administrative expenses in fiscal year 2012 were approximately 3 percent.[23] As we have previously concluded, because there are differences in which activities are defined as administrative costs for financial reporting purposes, a program with high administrative spending is not necessarily less efficient than a program with low administrative spending.[24] Programs with higher administrative cost caps may be assumed—incorrectly—to have higher administrative costs; so it is important to have an understanding of individual caps in place before any cross program comparisons are made.

There is no government-wide definition of what constitutes an administrative cost. Programs have different missions, priorities, services, and clients, and jurisdiction for the programs are often spread among numerous congressional committees; federal agencies' definitions of allowable (or prohibited) administrative costs vary from program to program. Additionally, the definition of administrative costs varies across different federal grant programs even though many of the same activities are performed.25 For example, the salary of an enrollment specialist at Head Start, who enrolls children in the program, is considered a program-related cost. However, the salary of similar position as an intake specialist for the Low Income Home Energy Assistance Program, who determines the eligibility and benefit level for participants, may be an administrative cost in some states where the program is administered.26 When the same expenses are treated differently across programs, this results in different administrative cost totals for similar functions. Regardless of the reasons for variation in definitions of these costs, the existence of differences in definitions limits their comparability.27 Monitoring programs entails collection and use of program-related operational and financial data, but for information to be effective for decision making, it has to be pertinent to the individual program. OMB staff we spoke with stated that collecting grant administrative cost information government-wide would not identify whether funds for administrative costs are being spent effectively. Specifically, they told us that analysis of administrative costs and the identification of potential administrative cost savings should occur at the program level. They said that when comparing administrative costs across programs it is important to remember that some programs are inherently more expensive to administer than others.

Comparing unlike costs across different programs would lead to erroneous comparisons. However, comparisons of costs may be more appropriate when comparing programs that fulfill similar missions or provide similar services. Additionally, different definitions for administrative costs could present a challenge in situations when multiple grant programs are consolidated into one program.[28]

CONCLUDING OBSERVATIONS

Administrative activities—such as reporting on project status, managing finances, and ensuring quality—are an essential part of the grant process. Selected programs track administrative costs in different ways and not all of the grant programs we reviewed have systems in place that could readily aggregate these costs from their grant recipients. Additionally, the actual cost of administering a given program may be paid by sources other than the federal government and the current collection of grant administrative cost data only reflects the federally reimbursed portion of these costs. Efficient and effective use of federal grant funds has always been important, but attention to the balance between program costs and administrative costs grows as budgets come under increasing pressures and the resources available for achieving federal grants' goals become further constrained. Although looking at administrative costs may seem like a logical first step when identifying opportunities to reduce expenses in such a budgetary environment, our review identified a number of factors that hinder the comparability of administrative costs across grant programs. Differences in cost caps and definitions are among the most important of these factors and make comparisons across grant programs very challenging, particularly when comparing programs with diverse missions and objectives. Comparing dissimilar costs leads to inappropriate conclusions that may have a perverse impact on federal policy making.

Comparisons of costs may be appropriate when reviewing programs that fulfill similar missions or provide similar service. However, comparisons of administrative costs across grant programs that provide different services should be made with caution. Any comparisons of administrative cost data should consider variation in administrative cost caps and cost definitions.

AGENCY COMMENTS AND OUR EVALUATION

We provided a draft of this report to the Secretary of the Department of Health and Human Services and the Secretary of the Department of Housing and Urban Development. The Department of Health and Human Services had technical comments, which we incorporated as appropriate. The Department of Housing and Urban Development did not provide comments. We also provided an informational copy to the Director of the Office of Management and Budget.

Susan J. Irving
Director for Federal Budget Analysis, Strategic Issues

APPENDIX I: OBJECTIVES, SCOPE, AND METHODOLOGY

This report examines (1) the extent to which selected federal agencies and grantees have mechanisms and guidance in place to distinguish between administrative and program costs and to facilitate the availability of these data to Congress and the public; and (2) the extent to which there are challenges that hinder the comparability of grant administrative cost data. To address these objectives, we selected two agencies for our review—the Departments of Health and Human Services (HHS) and Housing and Urban Development (HUD). HHS manages the largest share of federal grant making both in terms of grant obligation amount and the number of grant programs. We included HUD to obtain management perspectives on a different set of programs and issues.[1] Collectively, the selected agencies provide diversity in the number of grant programs and grant obligations and management perspectives on administrative and program costs.

At each selected agency, we identified three programs that provided a combination of the high dollar grant obligation in fiscal year 2012 and different grant types, such as project and formula, as well as grantee type, including state and local government and nonprofit and for-profit entities. [2] At HHS we selected the following grant programs: (1) Child Care and Development Fund; (2) Head Start; and (3) Allergy, Immunology and Transplantation Research. At HUD we selected the following grant programs: (1) HOME Investment Partnerships Program; (2) Community Development Block Grant; and (3) Multifamily Housing Service Coordinators. There were certain programs that met the criterion of high grant obligation at each selected agency but we did not consider them for selection for one or more reasons, including: administrative features of the grant program that made them unique and distinctly atypical of the grants at these agencies or planned consolidation of the program that made the review less relevant.

To determine the extent to which selected federal agencies and grantees have mechanisms and guidance in place to distinguish between administrative and program costs, we reviewed each program's authorizing statutes and regulations, where applicable, program guidance, and grant documents. We interviewed agency officials responsible for each of the selected grant programs to understand how these programs collect grant administrative cost data, the type of guidance, training, and technical assistance they provide grantees, and their requirements and experiences with determining and reporting administrative costs. To inform our work on government-wide efforts to collect grant administrative cost information, we interviewed staff at the Office of Management and Budget's (OMB) Office of Federal Financial Management, which oversees the financial management policy of the federal government.

To examine the extent to which there are challenges that hinder the comparability of grant administrative cost data we performed work at the primary recipient level.

Based on fiscal year 2012 grant obligation data for selected grant programs to state and local governments from OMB's Analytical Perspectives, we selected two states—Massachusetts, which receives a relatively high amount of federal grant funds and was in the top quarter of fiscal year 2012 federal grant obligations, and New Hampshire, which receives a relatively low amount of federal grant funds and was in the bottom quarter of fiscal year 2012 federal grant obligations. We then selected primary grant recipients within those states with the highest grant obligation for each selected grant program.

We next confirmed USASpending grant obligation amounts with HHS and HUD officials. We subsequently replaced certain primary grant recipients that had met the criteria of highest grant obligation for each selected grant program within the selected states because we determined that USASpending did not fully or correctly identify the grantee. Although the results of our review are not generalizable to other grant programs in other agencies, they are indicative of the wide variation associated with the mechanisms and guidance for tracking grant administrative costs and the utility of these costs for program management.

We conducted a literature review to identify issues raised, including those in our previous reports as well as the Congressional Research Service and the Congressional Budget Office, related to grant administrative costs, grants management, and cost principles. Additionally, we reviewed research reports from research groups and state representative organizations that discuss grant administrative costs from the perspective of grantees. We reviewed relevant HHS and HUD websites and related agency documents to understand grant administrative costs guidance for selected grant programs.

We conducted this performance audit from January 2014 to December 2014 in accordance with generally accepted government auditing standards. Those standards require that we plan and perform the audit to obtain sufficient, appropriate evidence to provide a reasonable basis for our findings and conclusions based on our audit objectives. We believe that the evidence obtained provides a reasonable basis for our findings and conclusions based on our audit objectives.

APPENDIX II: SELECTED GRANT PROGRAMS, ADMINISTRATIVE COSTS CAPS, AND ADMINISTRATIVE COST DEFINITIONS

Program name	Administrative cost cap	Types of expenses included in administrative cost caps
HOME Investment Partnerships Program	10%	Includes program planning costs and salaries of participating jurisdiction's staff who perform activities, including compliance, developing interagency agreements, monitoring of HOME-assisted housing, reporting to HUD, program evaluation, audit resolution, providing public information, and travel costs; third-party audit, legal and accounting services; rental and purchase of equipment, insurance, utilities, office supplies and office space; the costs of administering tenant-based rental assistance programs; and indirect costs.
Community Development Block Grant (CDBG)	20%	Includes program planning costs and salaries of staff who perform activities, including providing information to the public, preparing budgets, monitoring and compliance, developing interagency agreements, preparing reports for HUD, audit resolution, program evaluation and supervising employees engaged in thesame; travel costs incurred for official business; third-party legal, accounting and audit services; rental or purchase of equipment, insurance, utilities; office supplies and office space; and indirect costs.
Multifamily Housing Service Coordinators	None	No applicable regulatory or statutory definitions.
Child Care and Development Fund (CCDF)	5% (15% for Indian tribes)	Includes salaries of administrative and implementation agency staff; costs related to planning, developing, and designing the program; public outreach and hearings; preparing the application; monitoring and reporting on program activities; coordinating with federal, state and local officials; official travel; accounting and audit services; rental and purchase of equipment, utilities, and office supplies; and indirect costs.
Head Start	15%	Includes costs related to overall management, including salaries of the executive director, personnel officer, fiscal officer/bookkeeper, payroll/insurance/property clerk, and janitor for administrative office space, and costs associated with volunteers carrying out administrative functions; fringe benefits, travel, transportation and

Program name	Administrative cost cap	Types of expenses included in administrative cost caps
		training; expenses related to bookkeeping and payroll services, audits, and bonding; administrative office insurance, supplies, copy machines, postage, and utilities; and occupying, operating and maintaining space for administrative activities.
Allergy, Immunology and Transplantation Research (AITR)	26%[a]	Indirect charges that typically include depreciation on buildings and equipment; costs of operating such facilities; salaries of executive officers attributable to administrative functions; salaries of clerical staff; office supplies; and library expenses.

Source: GAO analysis of HUD and HHS program regulations.

[a] AITR grantees do not have statutory or individual program administrative cost caps. However, OMB Circular No. A-21 (now codified in Title 2 of the Code of Federal Regulations) imposes a 26 percent cap on administrative (but not facilities) expenses for universities. Costs for administration are limited to 26 percent of total direct costs.

End Notes

1 Office of Management and Budget, Analytical Perspectives, Budget of the United States Government, Fiscal Year 2015 (Washington, D.C.: 2014). Federal outlay data for fiscal year 2013 reflects the most current available data at the time of this report. These data include grants to states for Medicaid, the federal government's largest single grant program.

2 Pub. L. No. 113-101, 128 Stat. 1146 (May 9, 2014). The DATA Act is intended to increase accountability and transparency of federal spending and requires federal agencies to publicly report, on at least a quarterly basis, certain information about any funding made available to, or expended by, an agency or component of the agency. This requires a variety of information on the appropriation account, including budget authority, obligations, unobligated balances, outlays, and any other budget resources—at different levels of aggregation and disaggregation: appropriations account, program activities, and object classification. The DATA Act also provides for the establishment of government-wide financial data standards to, among other things, produce consistent and comparable data across program activities. Reporting is required to begin no later than May 9, 2017 (3 years after enactment).

3 This information was highlighted in a Data Transparency Town Hall meeting hosted by Treasury and OMB on September 26, 2014.

4 In early 2014, the House passed a bill that would require agencies to provide additional program-level information to be reported publicly, including total administrative costs of programs. See Taxpayers Right-To-Know Act, H.R. 1423, 113th Cong. (2014).

5 Office of Management and Budget, Analytical Perspectives, Budget of the United States Government, Fiscal Year 2014 (Washington, D.C.: 2013).

[6] GAO reports include: Biomedical Research: NIH Should Assess the Impact of Growth in Indirect Costs on Its Mission, GAO-13-760 (Washington, D.C.: Sept. 24, 2013); Community Development Block Grants: Reporting on Compliance with Limit on Funds Used for Administration Can Be Improved, GAO-13-247 (Washington, D.C.: Mar. 21, 2013); Grants to State and Local Governments: An Overview of Federal Funding Levels and Selected Challenges, GAO-12-1016 (Washington, D.C.: Sept. 25, 2012); University Research: Policies for the Reimbursement of Indirect Costs Need to Be Updated, GAO-10-937 (Washington, D.C.: Sept. 8, 2010); Nonprofit Sector: Treatment and Reimbursement of Indirect Costs Vary among Grants, and Depend Significantly on Federal, State, and Local Government Practices, GAO-10-477 (Washington, D.C.: May 18, 2010); Human Service Programs: Demonstration Projects Could Identify Ways to Simplify Policies and Facilitate Technology Enhancements to Reduce Administrative Costs, GAO-06-942 (Washington, D.C.: Sept. 19, 2006); Budget Issues: Assessing Executive Order 12837 on Reducing Administrative Expenses, GAO/AIMD-94-15 (Washington, D.C.: Nov. 17, 1993).

[7] An entity may establish an indirect cost rate by submitting a proposal to its cognizant rate-setting agency. For educational institutions, this is determined by which federal agency provides the greatest amount of funds to the entity for the most recent 3 years— using a base year that represents historical costs by fiscal year. After the proposal has been reviewed or audited, the cognizant rate-setting agency and the school negotiate and come to agreement on the rate. The rate is then documented in a formal indirect cost rate agreement. See GAO-10-937.

[8] GAO has analyzed the indirect cost reimbursement procedures for higher education institutions previously. See GAO-10-937.

[9] GAO, Homelessness: Information on Administrative Costs for HUD's Emergency Shelter Grants Program, GAO-10-491 (Washington, D.C.: May 20, 2010).

[10] GAO-10-477.

[11] The Urban Institute, Nonprofit-Government Contracts and Grants: Findings from the 2013 National Survey (December 2013). In 2013, the Urban Institute surveyed nonprofit organizations regarding their experiences with government contracts and grants. This survey was based on a national, randomly drawn sample of 501(c)(3) public charities taken from the Urban Institute's National Center for Charitable Statistics. The sample was limited to organizations that are required to file a Form 990 (an annual financial statement) with the U.S. Internal Revenue Service and have more than $100,000 in expenditures. A total of 4,024 nonprofit organizations completed the survey and of that number 2,764 indicated they had government contracts and grants.

[12] OMB guidance is applicable to all grant programs and provides policies to be followed by the grant-making agency, not grantee. The grant-making agencies codify OMB's guidance into their own grant regulations, which then make them binding on the grantee.

[13] 78 Fed. Reg. 78,590 (Dec. 26, 2013). OMB's final guidance was published in Title 2, subtitle A, of the Code of Federal Regulations and consolidated eight grants management circulars, including: A–21 (Cost Principles for Educational Institutions), A–87 (Cost Principles for State, Local and Indian Tribal Governments), A–110 (Uniform Administrative Requirements for Grants and Agreements With Institutions of Higher Education, Hospitals, and Other Non-Profit Organizations), A–122 (Cost Principles for Non-Profit Organizations), A–89 (Federal Domestic Assistance Program Information), A–102 (Grants and Cooperative Agreements with State and Local Governments), A–133 (Audits of States, Local Governments and Non-Profit Organizations), and A–50 (Audit Follow-up).

[14] The new Uniform Guidance also establishes a de minimis indirect cost rate of 10 percent of Modified Total Direct Costs, which means all direct salaries and wages, applicable fringe benefits, materials and supplies, services, travel, and subawards and subcontracts up to the first $25,000 of each subaward or subcontract. This allows nonfederal grantees who have never had a negotiated indirect cost rate to receive indirect costs without the administrative burden associated with applying for, and receiving, such a rate.

[15] OMB staff explained that they do not have a mechanism in place to collect that data centrally across all federal agencies.

[16] 31 U.S.C. §§ 7501-7507. The Single Audit Act, as amended, requires each federal entity that expends a certain amount of federal awards, including grants and other assistance, in a fiscal year to have a single or program-specific audit conducted by an independent auditor. The audit includes the entity's financial statements and a schedule of expenditures of federal awards, and a review of related internal controls. OMB sets the threshold for reporting. From 2004 to 2014, the threshold requiring a single or program-specific audit is $500,000. The new OMB Uniform Guidance, effective for grantees on December 26, 2014 has increased the Single Audit threshold to $750,000 or more in federal fund expenditures.

[17] The Federal Financial Report (Standard Form-425) is used for reporting grant expenditures for the recipients of federal funding assistance.

[18] For example, OMB guidance on cost principles for educational institutions states that the salaries of administrative and clerical staff should normally be treated as Facilities and Administrative costs. Direct charging of these costs may be appropriate where a major project or activity explicitly budgets for administrative or clerical services and individuals involved can be specifically identified with the project or activity. "Major project" is defined as a project that requires an extensive amount of administrative or clerical support, which is significantly greater than the routine level of such services provided by academic departments.

[19] AITR's guidance is available in the NIH Grants Policy Statement available on NIH's grants management website. CCDF provides its resources on the Administration for Children and Families site, while CDBG and HOME resources are provided via HUD's OneCPD.

[20] Urban Institute, Nonprofit-Government Contracts and Grants: Findings from the 2013 National Survey, (December 2013).

[21] CCDF has a 5 percent administrative cost cap that applies to states and territories and a 15 percent administrative cost cap for tribal communities.

[22] See appendix II for applicable administrative cost caps and the types of expenses they include. Three of the programs we reviewed, HOME, CCDF, and Head Start, have a cost cap established by authorizing statutes and are included in the program regulations. CDBG has an administrative cost cap established in its appropriations and program regulations. While the AITR grant does not have a program-specific administrative cost cap, a cap may exist depending on the type of organization that receives the award. The MHSC grant program has no cap for administrative costs and does not have any program-specific regulations regarding administrative costs.

[23] CDBG data are based on expenditures. Compliance with the CDGB administrative cap for entitlement communities is based on obligated funds. GAO issued a recommendation related to this in GAO-13-247.

[24] GAO-06-942.

[25] GAO-06-942. In 2006, we reviewed seven programs from HHS and the Departments of Agriculture and Labor and found that the statutes and regulations for the programs define administrative costs differently even though many of the same activities were performed.

[26] States may only use 10 percent of federal funds for planning and administering the Low Income Home Energy Assistance Program. The program's regulations do not define "costs of planning and administration" and therefore states vary in how they interpret these costs in determining their administrative expenses. Sample definitions for administrative costs include all costs associated with management oversight of the program, including participant eligibility for assistance. States are considered the primary interpreters and HHS defers to the state definitions unless they are considered clearly erroneous. This variation could be the result of a difference in the complexity in determining applicant eligibility, the amount of interaction with beneficiaries, as well as the overall nature of the programs.

[27] GAO-06-942.

[28] For more information on grant consolidations, see GAO, Grant Program Consolidations: Lessons Learned and Implications for Congressional Oversight, GAO-15-125 (Washington, D.C.: Dec. 12, 2014).

End Notes for Appendix I

[1] To determine which agencies had high grant obligation amounts we used USASpending data for fiscal year 2012 and to determine which agencies had a high volume of grant programs we used program counts from the Catalog of Federal Domestic Assistance.

[2] A formula grant is allocated to eligible recipients based on formula factors, such as state population, established in statutory and regulatory provisions. A project grant provides funding for fixed or known periods of specific projects.

In: Federal Grant Management and Controls ISBN: 978-1-63482-559-7
Editor: Dana T. Greer

Chapter 3

RECOVERY ACT: GRANT IMPLEMENTATION EXPERIENCES OFFER LESSONS FOR ACCOUNTABILITY AND TRANSPARENCY[*]

United States Government Accountability Office

WHY GAO DID THIS STUDY

In response to the recent serious recession, Congress enacted the Recovery Act to promote economic recovery, make investments, and minimize or avoid reductions in state and local government services. Approximately $219 billion was distributed as grants for use in states and localities, making grants a major component of the act. These grants covered a broad range of areas including education, transportation, energy, infrastructure, the environment, health care, and housing.

GAO was asked to examine grant management lessons learned resulting from the Recovery Act. This report examines federal, state, and local experiences with implementing grants funded by the Recovery Act by identifying examples of good practices employed and challenges faced in meeting the act's accountability and transparency requirements. GAO reviewed relevant documents including OMB and Recovery Board guidance, relevant literature, and previous reports by GAO, federal inspectors general,

---

[*] This is an edited, reformatted and augmented version of a United States Government Accountability Office publication, No. GAO-14-219, dated January 2014.

and others. GAO also interviewed officials from OMB, the Recovery Board, four federal agencies, three state governments, and two local governments, among others. This report also draws on GAO's past bimonthly reviews of selected states' and localities' use of Recovery funds.

WHAT GAO RECOMMENDS

GAO is not making any recommendations in this report. We provided a draft of this report to relevant agencies for comment. They generally agreed with our findings and provided technical comments.

WHAT GAO FOUND

Federal, state, and local officials responsible for implementing grants funded by the American Recovery and Reinvestment Act of 2009 (Recovery Act) as well as the external oversight community reported lessons learned regarding both useful practices and challenges to ensuring accountability. Faced with aggressive timelines for distributing billions of dollars, they adopted a number of practices to foster accountability including (1) strong support by top leaders; (2) centrally-situated collaborative governance structures; (3) the use of networks and agreements to share information and work towards common goals; and (4) adjustments to, and innovations in, usual approaches to conducting oversight such as the increased use of up-front risk assessments, the gathering of "real time" information, earlier communication of audit findings, and the use of advanced data analytics. For example, in 2009, the Recovery Accountability and Transparency Board (Recovery Board) established the Recovery Operations Center which used advanced data analysis techniques to identify potential fraud and errors before and after payments were made. The Recovery Act's emphasis on accountability also presented challenges for several states and federal agencies. These included limited resources for oversight at the state and local levels, and the speed with which Recovery Act funds were distributed. One state addressed the challenge of limited resources by transferring funds from its central administration account to Recovery Act oversight. To facilitate the quick distribution of funds, maintenance-of-effort provisions concerning transportation projects (which prevented Recovery funds from being used for planned state projects) were rolled out before the Department of Transportation had time to issue sufficiently detailed definitions of what constituted "state funding." To address this challenge, the department had to issue clarifying guidance to states seven times during the first year of the Recovery Act.

Federal, state, and local officials also developed practices and encountered challenges related to the transparency of Recovery Act funds. An example of one good practice that was required by the Recovery Act was the creation of the Recovery.gov website. This site, as well as similar portals created by states and localities, demonstrated several leading practices for effective government websites. These included (1) establishing a clear purpose, (2) using social networking tools to garner interest, (3) tailoring the website to meet audience needs, and (4) obtaining stakeholder input during design. Efforts to increase transparency also led to challenges for several states and federal agencies. For example, some recipients lacked knowledge or expertise in using the data systems needed to report grant spending, while others faced challenges with reporting the same data to multiple systems. Early GAO reviews also found several problems with job reporting data including discrepancies in how full time equivalents were recorded and the capacity of recipients to meet reporting deadlines. The Office of Management and Budget (OMB) addressed these challenges by issuing additional guidance and providing technical support. Finally, agencies receiving Recovery Act funds were required to submit performance plans that identified measures on a program-by-program basis. The level of detail and the specificity of outcomes in these plans varied greatly for the agencies GAO examined, making it difficult to determine the extent to which some were making progress toward their goals and demonstrating results.

ABBREVIATIONS

ARRA	American Recovery and Reinvestment Act of 2009
API	Application Program Interface
BCN	ARRA Big City Network
CBO	Congressional Budget Office
DOE	Department of Energy
HUD	Department of Housing and Urban Development
DOT	Department of Transportation
FHWA	Federal Highway Administration
FTE	Full-time Equivalent

GPRAMA	GRPA Modernization Act of 2010
IG	Inspector General
MASSPIRG	Massachusetts Public Interest Research Group
NIAF	National Intergovernmental Audit Forum
NRT	National Review Team
OMB	Office of Management and Budget
Recovery Board	Recovery Accountability and Transparency Board
ROC	Recovery Operations Center
SFSF	State Fiscal Stabilization Fund

* * *

January 24, 2014

The Honorable Thomas R. Carper
Chairman
The Honorable Tom Coburn, M.D.
Ranking Member
Committee on Homeland Security and Governmental Affairs
United States Senate

The Honorable Claire McCaskill
Chairman
Subcommittee on Financial and Contracting Oversight
Committee on Homeland Security and Governmental Affairs
United States Senate

In response to the recent serious recession, Congress enacted the American Recovery and Reinvestment Act of 2009 (Recovery Act) to, among other purposes, promote economic recovery, make investments, and minimize and avoid reductions in state and local government services.[1] A significant component of the Recovery Act was grants for use in states and localities. As of the end of October 2013, the Department of the Treasury had awarded approximately $219 billion of Recovery Act funds in the form of grants. These grants covered a broad range of areas including education, transportation, infrastructure, energy, the environment, health care, and housing. The importance of spending Recovery Act funds quickly was highlighted by the President's goal of spending 70 percent of the funds by September 30, 2010. You asked us to examine grant management lessons learned resulting from the

Recovery Act and to provide examples of what worked well, as well as what challenges were experienced by federal, state, and local governments.

To better understand grant management lessons learned resulting from the Recovery Act, we focused on two key issues involving grant implementation—accountability[2] and transparency[3]—where Congress and the administration placed unprecedented emphasis when they crafted the Recovery Act. Specifically, this report identifies and provides examples of good practices employed and the challenges faced in meeting the Recovery Act's accountability and transparency requirements by select federal, state, and local agencies implementing grant programs funded by the Recovery Act. Additionally, in September 2013, we issued a related report examining federal efforts to increase the transparency of federal data and identifying lessons learned from operating existing data systems that could contribute to these efforts.[4]

To accomplish our objectives, we conducted a detailed literature review to identify relevant prior work by us and others regarding Recovery Act challenges and lessons learned.[5] We then interviewed federal, state, and local officials involved in the implementation of the Recovery Act and obtained supporting documentation. The federal entities that we contacted with broad jurisdiction for the Recovery Act were the Recovery Implementation Office, the Office of Management and Budget (OMB), and the Recovery Accountability and Transparency Board (Recovery Board).[6] We developed criteria to select a subset of four federal agencies, three state governments, and two local governments. We then contacted these entities in order to obtain a more in-depth understanding of their experiences with grant programs funded by the Recovery Act as well as to identify examples of challenges and good practices. Our selection criteria included factors such as the nature, type, and value of the grants handled by the organization; whether the grants involved were already well-established, greatly increased in size, or entirely new; and the extent to which the organizations were identified in our previous work or in the broader literature. The federal agencies we selected were the Departments of Education, Energy, Transportation, and Housing and Urban Development. We deemed Medicaid out of scope for the purposes of this review. Although it was the largest grant program funded by the Recovery Act, it is primarily an entitlement and is subject to specific rules that are not typical of program grants.

The state and local governments we selected included California, Georgia, and Massachusetts, as well as New York, New York and Denver, Colorado. These three states are part of a core group of 16 states and the District of

Columbia that we selected for our series of bimonthly reviews of how Recovery Act funds were being used by recipients. The Recovery Act required that we conduct these bimonthly reviews of how these funds were used by selected states and localities. This report also fulfills this requirement in that we examined the use of Recovery Act funds in the previously mentioned states and cities. To obtain a broader state perspective, we interviewed officials from the state Recovery Act coordinators' network, which included key state officials responsible for implementing the Recovery Act from several states. For additional context, we supplemented these interviews by meeting with officials from state and local advocacy organizations such as the National Association of State Auditors and Comptrollers; the National Association of State Budget Officers; and the National Association of Counties. We reviewed and synthesized the information provided by these officials, as well as previously issued work regarding challenges and good practices that relate to our two key themes, and we developed descriptive examples. We also reviewed and applied criteria established by HowTo.gov, a source of guidance and leading practices for government websites, to Recovery.gov and state and local Recovery websites. A full description of our objectives, scope, and methodology is provided in appendix I.

We conducted this performance audit from December 2012 to January 2014 in accordance with generally accepted government auditing standards. Those standards require that we plan and perform the audit to obtain sufficient, appropriate evidence to provide a reasonable basis for our findings and conclusions based on our audit objectives. We believe that the evidence obtained provides a reasonable basis for our findings and conclusions based on our audit objectives.

BACKGROUND

The stated purposes of the Recovery Act are to:

- preserve and create jobs and promote economic recovery;
- assist those most impacted by the recession;
- provide investments needed to increase economic efficiency by spurring technological advances in science and health;
- invest in transportation, environmental protection, and other infrastructure that will provide long-term economic benefits; and

- stabilize state and local government budgets, in order to minimize and avoid reductions in essential services and counterproductive state and local tax increases.[7]

While many Recovery Act projects focused on immediately jumpstarting the economy, some projects—such as those involving investments in technology, infrastructure, and the environment—are expected to contribute to economic growth for many years.

The Recovery Act established the Recovery Accountability and Transparency Board (Recovery Board) to provide additional monitoring and oversight. The board was originally scheduled to terminate operations by September 30, 2013,[8] but its mission has been extended until September 30, 2015, to provide oversight and monitoring of assistance provided in response to Hurricane Sandy, which hit the northeast in October 2012.[9] The timeline in figure 1 displays selected events related to the Recovery Act and its requirements.

Recovery Act Funding

The Congressional Budget Office (CBO) initially estimated the cost of the Recovery Act to be approximately $787 billion; however, CBO's most recent estimate projects that the Recovery Act will cost approximately $830 billion over the 2009-2019 time period.[10] As of October 31, 2013, the federal government provided a total of approximately $812 billion related to Recovery Act activities. This includes funding to 28 federal agencies that were distributed to states, localities, and other entities; individuals through a combination of tax benefits and cuts; entitlements; and loans, contracts, and grants. See figure 2 for an overview of Recovery Act spending by category and program. Although Medicaid was the single largest Recovery Act grant program, we did not include it in our review because it is primarily an entitlement program and subject to specific rules that are not typical of program grants.[11] Accordingly, we included the Recovery Act funds directed to Medicaid in the entitlement category, rather than the grant category, in figure 2. Emphasizing the importance of spending Recovery Act funds quickly, the President established a goal that by September 30, 2010, 70 percent of Recovery Act funding should be spent (that is, both obligated and outlayed).[12] Therefore, agencies had approximately 19 months to spend almost three-quarters of their Recovery funds.

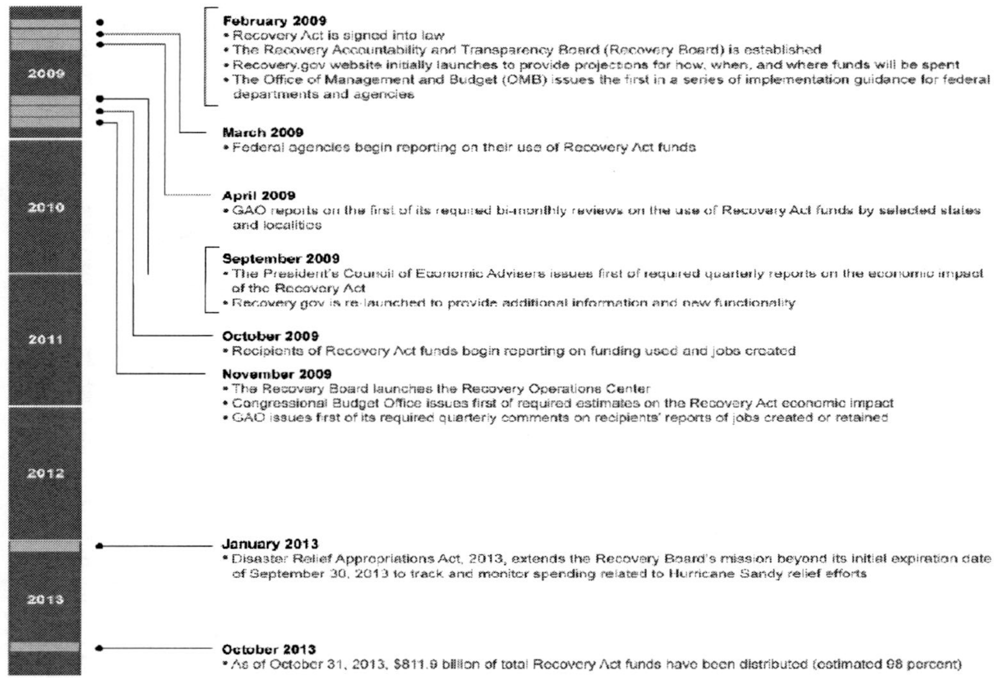

Source: GAO presentation of information from Congressional Budget Office, Office of Management and Budget, Recovery Board, and the White House.

Figure 1. Timeline of Selected Recovery Act Events.

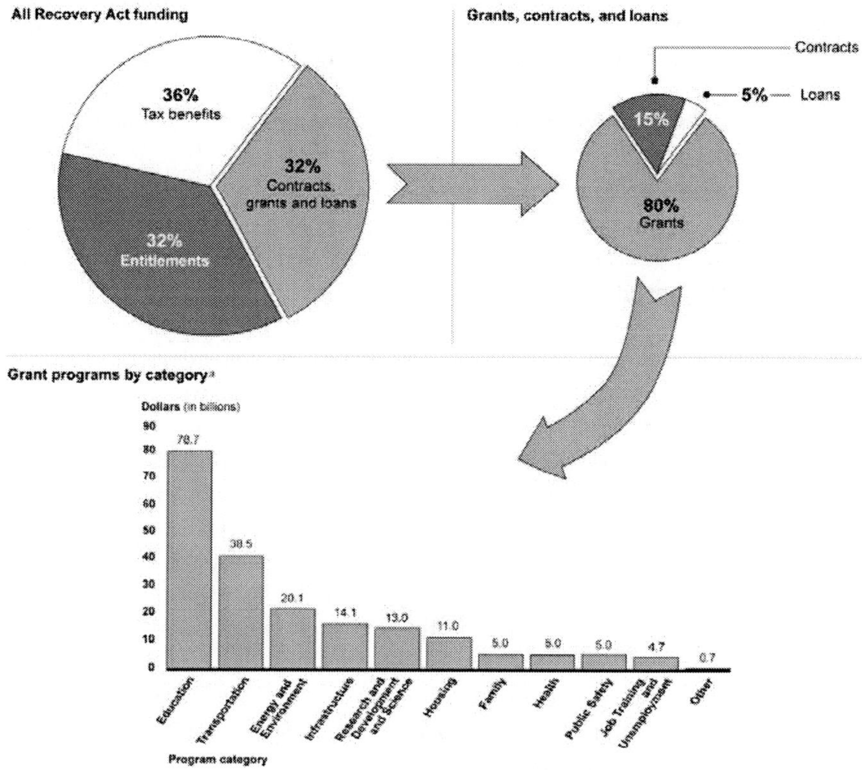

Source: GAO analysis of Recovery.gov, U.S. Treasury Federal Agency Financial and Activity Raports and Recovery Act recipient reporting data.

[a]Does not include Medicaid which is instead reflected in the entitlement category in the first pie chart above.

Figure 2. Overview of Recovery Act Spending by Program and Category, as of October 31, 2013.

Grant Programs Funded by the Recovery Act

Grants have played a key role in providing Recovery Act funds to recipients, with approximately $219 billion being awarded for use in states and localities through a wide variety of federal grant programs. With the intent of disbursing funds quickly to create and retain jobs and stabilize state and local budgets, a large majority of Recovery Act grant funding went to states and localities within 3 years of the law's enactment. Recipients reported receiving approximately 88 percent of their grant awards by the end of the 2nd quarter of calendar year 2013. State and local spending was as follows:

- Fiscal year 2009: spending totaled approximately $53 billion in actual outlays.
- Fiscal year 2010: spending was at its highest level with approximately $112 billion in actual outlays.
- Fiscal year 2011: spending decreased from its peak, with approximately $69 billion in actual outlays.

The 28 federal agencies that received Recovery funds developed specific plans for spending the money.[13] The agencies then awarded grants and contracts to state governments or, in some cases, directly to schools, hospitals, or other entities. OMB guidance directed these federal agencies to file weekly financial reports detailing how the money was being distributed. Recipients of the funds, in turn, were required by the Recovery Act to file quarterly reports on how they were spending the Recovery Act funds that they received.

Recovery Act grants provided to states and localities covered a broad range of areas such as transportation, energy, and housing. Education programs were the largest recipients of Recovery Act grant awards. Of the education programs funded in the Recovery Act, the largest in terms of funding was the newly created State Fiscal Stabilization Fund (SFSF) program, which provided assistance to state governments to stabilize their budgets by minimizing budgetary cuts in education and other essential government services, such as public safety. The Recovery Act appropriated $53.6 billion for the SFSF program.[14] As figure 2 (above) shows, grants represent over one-quarter of Recovery Act funding. Out of that category, funding received in the program areas of education, transportation, and energy and environment amount to approximately $137 billion, or 70 percent, of Recovery Act grant spending to date.

Recovery Act Oversight and Accountability Responsibilities of Key Participants

The Recovery Act called for a large amount of federal funds to be spent (that is, obligated and outlayed) in a short period of time—approximately 19 months—by the end of September 30, 2010. To assure the public that their tax dollars were being spent efficiently and effectively, the Recovery Act placed increased emphasis on accountability and transparency through enhanced reporting, auditing, and evaluation requirements for users of Recovery Act funds. The Recovery Act delineated some of these increased accountability and transparency responsibilities to existing organizations and entities as well as newly-created ones. See table 1 for details regarding the primary accountability and oversight responsibilities of key organizations involved in implementing the Recovery Act.

Table 1. Key Organizations and Their Primary Accountability and Oversight Responsibilities Regarding Implementation of the Recovery Act

Key organizations and entities	**Primary accountability and oversight responsibilities**
Federal government	
Congressional Budget Office	• Provide periodic estimates on the Recovery Act's effect on employment. *(Recovery Act, div. A, § 1512(e), 123 Stat. at 288)*
Council of Economic Advisers	• Prepare periodic reports on employment and economic impacts of Recovery Act spending. *(Recovery Act, div. A, § 1513, 123 Stat. at 288)*
Federal agencies	• Report how they are distributing the funds on a weekly basis. *(Office of Management and Budget Guidance, OMB Memorandum M-09-10)* • Use a separate accounting identifier for Recovery Act funded projects. *(Office of Management and Budget Guidance, OMB Memorandum M-09-10)* • Make publicly available recipient reports within 30 days of the end of each quarter. *(Recovery Act, div. A, § 1512(d), 123 Stat. at 288)*15
Government Accountability Office	• Conduct bimonthly reviews and prepare reports of such reviews ofselected states' and localities' use of Recovery Act funds. *(Recovery Act, div A, § 901(a), 123 Stat. at 191)* • Comment on quarterly recipient reports on the number of jobs created or preserved. *(Recovery Act, div. A, § 1512(e), 123 Stat. at 288)* •Review areas such as trade adjustment assistance, new education incentive grants, and efforts to increase small business lending. *(Recovery Act, div. B, § 1894, 123 Stat. at 423, Recovery Act, div. A, § 14009, 123 Stat. at. 285 and Recovery Act, div. A, § 507, Stat. at 158)*
Inspectors general	• Audit the programs, grants, and projects funded under the Recovery Act, both within their particular agency or department and collectively address concerns raised by the public. *(Recovery Act, div. A, § 1514, 123 Stat. 289)* • Serve on Recovery Act Board. *(Recovery Act, div. A, § 1522(b), 123 Stat. at 290)*16

Table 1. (Continued)

Key organizations and entities	Primary accountability and oversight responsibilities
	• Conduct whistleblower reprisal investigations. *(Recovery Act, div. A, 123 § 1553,Stat. 297)*
Office of Management and Budget (OMB)	• Coordinate with federal agencies on recipient reporting guidance. *(Recovery Act,div. A, § 1512(g), 123 Stat. at 288)* • Coordinate with the Council of Economic Advisers on their reports. *(Recovery Act, div. A, § 1513(a), 123 Stat. at 288)*
Recovery Accountability and Transparency Board (Recovery Board)	• Review whether use of Recovery Act funds met applicable standards and specified purposes. *(Recovery Act, div. A, § 1523(a)(2)(A), 123 Stat at 290)* • Identify fraud, waste and mismanagement related to the use of Recovery Act funds and refer to federal Inspector General. *(Recovery Act, div. A, § 1523(a)(1) and (a)(2)(C), 123 Stat at 290)* • Review whether there are sufficient and qualified contract and grant personnel overseeing Recovery Act funds. *(Recovery Act, div. A, § 1523(a)(2)(D), 123 Stat at 290)* • Submit quarterly and annual reports to the President and Congress, as well as "flash reports" on potential problems that require immediate attention.*(Recovery Act, div. A, § 1523(b)(1), (b)(2) and (b)(3), 123 Stat at 291)* • Make recommendations to federal agencies on measures to prevent fraud, waste, and mismanagement of Recovery Act funds. *(Recovery Act, div. A, § 1523(c)(1), 123 Stat at 291)* • Establish and maintain the Recovery.gov website. *(Recovery Act, div. A, § 1526(a), 123 Stat at 293)*
Recovery Implementation Office	• Support key administration officials and coordinate Recovery Act efforts at OMB. • Facilitate interagency coordination. • Complement oversight work led by the Recovery Board.
Recovery Independent Advisory Panel	• Provide recommendations to the Recovery Board to identify and prevent fraud, waste and abuse in Recovery Act programs. *(Recovery Act, div. A, § 1542, 123 Stat at 295)*
State government	
Governors	• Within 45 days of enactment of the Act, certify that the state will request and use funds provided by the Recovery Act and that the funds will be used to create jobs and promote economic growth. *(Recovery Act, div. A, § 1607(a), 123 Stat at303)*
State auditors	• Work with the Recovery Board in coordinating oversight activities. *(Recovery Act, div. A, § 1528, 123 Stat at 294)*
State government agencies	• Report on the amount of funds received on a quarterly basis. *(Recovery Act, div. A, § 1512 (c)(1), 123 Stat at 287)*

Key organizations and entities	**Primary accountability and oversight responsibilities**
	• Report on their use of funds on a quarterly basis. *(Recovery Act, div. A, § 1512(c)(2), 123 Stat at 287)* • Report on an estimate of the number of jobs created and the number of jobs retained on the quarterly basis. *(Recovery Act, div. A, § 1512(c)(3)(D), 123 Stat at 287)* • Use a separate accounting identifier for Recovery Act funded projects. *(Office of Management and Budget Guidance, OMB Memorandum M-09-10)*
Local government and others	
Recipients' of Recovery Act funds (local governments, universities and other research institutions, non-profit organizations, and private companies)	• Report quarterly on Recovery Act funds including on (1) the amount of funds received, (2) the amount of funds expended or obligated to projects and activities, (3) a detailed list of all projects and activities for which funds were expended or obligated, including a name, description, and evaluation of completion status for each project or activity, and (4) an estimate of the numberof jobs created and the number of jobs retained by each project or activity. *(Recovery Act, div. A § 1512(c), 123 Stat at 287-288)*

Source: GAO analysis of Recovery Act and OMB/White House memoranda.

PRACTICES AT FEDERAL, STATE, AND LOCAL LEVELS CONTRIBUTED TO IMPROVED ACCOUNTABILITY OF RECOVERY ACT GRANT PROGRAMS BUT CHALLENGES EXISTED

Strong Support by Top Leaders, a Collaborative Approach, and Systematic Use of Data Were Key to Managing Recovery Act Implementation

Under the Recovery Act, accountability for timely and effective implementation of the law was a shared responsibility that included agencies involved in directly implementing the law as well as the external oversight community. On the operational side, among the practices that facilitated accountability were (1) strong support by top leaders, (2) centrally-situated collaborative governance structures, and (3) the regular and systematic use of data to support management reviews.

Strong Support by Top Leaders

We have previously reported on the importance of having the active support of top leadership when undertaking large and complex activities.[17] This was the case in the implementation of the Recovery Act where, at the federal level, the President and Vice President made clear that effective Recovery Act implementation was a high priority for them. The President assigned overall management responsibility for the Recovery Act to the Vice President and appointed a former OMB deputy director to head the newly-created Recovery Implementation Office with direct reporting responsibilities to both him and the Vice President. The former head of the Recovery Implementation Office told us that his position gave him access to top leadership in the administration. This official said he participated in daily morning staff meetings with the White House senior staff, briefing them on any issues related to the Recovery Act. He briefed the President directly approximately once a month. In addition, he typically met with the Vice President's staff on a daily basis after the President's staff meeting. He also met with the Vice President directly every 1 to 2 weeks. Finally, he frequently interacted with the head of OMB and sometimes also sat in on his staff meetings.

In each of these roles he had direct access to, and support from, the highest levels of government. The former head of the Recovery Implementation Office stated this was key to his ability to ensure cooperation and coordination with other federal departments during the Recovery Act. For example, he told us that senior government leaders knew that his office had the authority of the President and Vice President behind it, and if they did not do what was requested, they would have to explain their reasoning to senior White House officials. This awareness of the Recovery Implementation Office's line of authority helped to ensure that federal officials coordinated and cooperated with the office. In turn, the involvement and engagement of top leaders at individual federal agencies was facilitated by OMB guidance that required each agency to identify a senior accountable official—generally at the deputy secretary or subcabinet level—to be responsible for Recovery planning, implementation, and performance activities within the agency.[18] These senior agency leaders were regularly involved with overseeing and reporting on Recovery Act efforts.

At the state level, several governors demonstrated top leadership support by establishing specific positions, offices, or both that were responsible for state Recovery efforts. For example, the Governor of Massachusetts created the Massachusetts Recovery and Reinvestment Office as a temporary program management office for the specific task of overseeing Recovery activities. The former director of the office stated that he reported directly to, and drew his authority from, the Governor. The Governor also elevated the office to the rank of a senior level office. This action increased the office's visibility and gave it a seat at the Governor's weekly cabinet meetings, where its director would regularly report on the status of Recovery Act projects. In addition, no state Recovery Act program could be approved without the director's consent. The former director told us that the success of the office was attributable to the direct line of authority it had with the Governor of Massachusetts. In fiscal year 2012, Massachusetts' Office of Commonwealth Performance, Accountability, and Transparency was created, in part, as a direct result of the Recovery Act. 19 According to Massachusetts' state officials, this office is the state's attempt to take lessons from the state's experience with the Massachusetts Recovery and Reinvestment Office and apply them post Recovery Act.

Centrally-Situated Collaborative Governance Structures

Collaboration played a key role in ensuring timely implementation of, and accountability for, Recovery Act grant programs. Because the success of the Recovery Act relied on many programs being implemented quickly at the federal, state, and local levels, cooperation and collaboration among these groups was essential. While centrally-situated federal entities such as the Recovery Implementation Office, OMB, and the Recovery Board set the tone, issued guidance, and provided ongoing oversight, many implementation decisions were left to state and local partners directly engaged in managing Recovery Act programs. For example, agencies and grantees were given freedom to publish notices of funding availability and to run competitions in a manner consistent with their individual statutes, regulations, and agency practices. On the other hand, there was also centralization of oversight as demonstrated by the direct involvement of high-level officials such as the Vice President, cabinet secretaries, and senior accountable officials in federal agencies receiving Recovery Act funding, as well as centrally-placed policy and oversight organizations such as OMB and the Recovery Board. This combination of a centralized and decentralized approach to managing the implementation of the Recovery Act represented a new method of managing grant oversight, one which simultaneously recognized the importance of collaboration while increasing the role of the center.[20]

Officials in the Recovery Implementation Office employed a collaborative, facilitative approach, while also leveraging the authority of the

Vice President to facilitate the participation of stakeholders. The office functioned as a convener and problem-solver that engaged with a wide range of federal, state and local partners. This approach was embodied in the objectives identified by the Vice President when the office was established. These objectives included the expectation that office staff respond to requests and questions within 24 hours, cut across bureaucratic silos by reaching out to a variety of partners, and always be accessible. Toward this end, the office adopted the role of an "outcome broker," working closely with partners across organizational silos at all levels of government in order to foster implementation of the Recovery Act and achieve results.[21] Another role of the Recovery Implementation Office was to closely monitor Recovery Act spending. One way it did so was to monitor grants to ensure that they were consistent with the objectives identified by the Vice President. A second way the office monitored spending was to review weekly financial reports on agency obligations and expenditures for programs receiving Recovery Act funds and to meet with the agencies on a regular basis.

OMB sought to facilitate effective implementation of the Recovery Act by working to establish and strengthen relationships with state and local governments that would ultimately implement the programs on the ground. This was done in two ways: (1) by soliciting feedback from state and local partners when formulating and revising rules and policies governing the implementation of Recovery Act programs and (2) by developing its capacity to respond to questions from the many states and localities that would be implementing those rules and policies. A senior OMB official directly involved in this work told us the office had to move out of its traditional role as mainly a policy-making organization to adopt a more interactive and service-oriented approach. Under this approach, key activities involved engaging with and obtaining feedback from states and localities as well as providing technical support to these groups so that they could meet the Recovery Act's numerous reporting requirements.

For example, to obtain feedback from state and local partners when developing key Recovery Act policies, OMB became actively involved in weekly conference calls that included a diverse group of federal, state, and local organizations. Starting in the spring of 2009, regular participants in these calls included OMB; GAO; the National Association of State Auditors, Comptrollers and Treasurers; the National Governors' Association; the National Association of State Budget Officers; the Recovery Board; the National Association of Counties; the National Association of State Chief Information Officers; and the National Association of State Purchasing

Officers. These weekly calls were scheduled after several of these organizations wrote to OMB and GAO to express their strong interest in coordinating on reporting and compliance aspects of the Recovery Act. An important outcome of this regular information exchange was to make OMB aware of the need to clarify certain reporting requirements. The Recovery Act required federal agencies to make information publicly available on the estimate of the number of jobs created and number of jobs retained as a result of activities funded by the act. Our previous Recovery Act work in the states raised the issue that some local officials needed clarification regarding definitions when reporting on job data. The local partners participating in these calls were able to corroborate what we reported and provide OMB with specific information about what additional guidance was needed. To obtain information to further guide refinements to the Recovery implementation process, at the end of 2009, OMB officials said they (1) interviewed and surveyed numerous stakeholders including governors and state and local recipients, and (2) worked with GAO to identify best practices. Based on these efforts, OMB subsequently revised its guidance, which focused on lessons learned around enhancing recipient reporting and compliance.[22]

To improve technical support provided to state and local governments implementing the Recovery Act, OMB worked with the Recovery Board to establish an assistance center based on an "incident command" model.[23] One OMB official likened this approach to an extension of a traditional response model used during natural disasters, where the country's economic condition during the Great Recession was the "incident" and the Recovery Act was the intervention to be rolled out through many partners. To help implement this approach, OMB worked with officials from the Department of Agriculture who offered the services of one of their national emergency management teams to help set up and coordinate this effort. Given the large number of state and local governments that needed to be supported, OMB requested that each agency with grant programs receiving Recovery Act funds contribute personnel to support the center. According to OMB officials, from September to mid-December of 2009, the center responded to approximately 35,000 questions from states and localities.

Regular and Systematic Use of Data to Support Management Reviews

Under the Recovery Act, some agencies used new data-driven approaches to inform how they managed programs, and some of those new approaches become institutionalized at the agencies post-Recovery. While the Government Performance and Results Act (GPRA) Modernization Act of

2010 (GPRAMA) laid out requirements for data-driven quarterly performance reviews, several Recovery Act efforts aided agencies in implementing those requirements. 24 For example, in February 2013 we found that the Department of Energy (DOE) built on its Recovery Act-related performance reviews and established quarterly performance reviews, called business quarterly reviews, in 2011.[25] Another control DOE implemented for large dollar projects was a "Stage-Gate" process, which did not allow the funds to be disbursed all at one time. It required the recipient to meet certain metrics before receiving additional funding at certain levels. DOE Office of Inspector General (OIG) officials believed this Stage-Gate approach was an effective internal control tool. Post-Recovery, DOE has institutionalized both the business quarterly reviews and Stage-Gate processes.

As part of the Department of Housing and Urban Development's (HUD) implementation of the Recovery Act, the agency piloted a new approach to data management and accountability called HUDStat. HUD's Recovery Act team collected data about the status of projects and progress towards financial goals. Armed with this information, HUD leaders could identify and neutralize spending delays across the agency's 80 field and regional offices. In some cases, a senior HUD official would make a phone call to a mayor or a governor to stress the need to spend funds quickly. In other cases, staff would refocus on regions where progress was slow and would work with grantees to move more quickly to promote economic growth. After the Recovery Act, and in accordance with GPRAMA requirements, HUD continued to use HUDStat to share data and resources across the agency.

Heightened Accountability Requirements and Aggressive Implementation Timelines Led to Increased Coordination and Information Sharing

The Recovery Act contained increased accountability requirements in the areas of reporting, audits, and evaluations to help ensure that tax dollars were being spent efficiently and effectively. At the same time, the act provided aggressive timelines—approximately 19 months—for the distribution of funds. The combination of these two factors placed high expectations on federal, state, and local governments and led to increased coordination both vertically across levels of government and horizontally within the same level of government to share information and work towards common goals.

Networks Provided a Mechanism to Share Information

Organizations involved in overseeing and implementing grants funded by the Recovery Act made use of both new and established networks to share information. Shortly after the Recovery Act was signed into law, our then Acting Comptroller General and the Chair of the Council of the Inspectors General on Integrity and Efficiency hosted a coordination meeting with the OIGs or their representatives from 17 federal agencies to discuss an approach to coordination and information sharing going forward. We also worked with state and local auditors and their associations to facilitate regular conference calls to discuss Recovery Act issues with a broad community of interested parties. Participants included the Association of Government Accountants; the Association of Local Government Auditors; the National Association of State Auditors, Comptrollers, and Treasurers; the Recovery Board; and federal OIGs.

Another active venue for information sharing was the National Intergovernmental Audit Forum (NIAF). The NIAF, led during this period by our then Acting Comptroller General, is an association that has existed for over three decades as a means for federal, state, and local audit executives to discuss issues of common interest and enhance accountability. NIAF's May 2009 meeting brought together these executives and others including OMB, to update them on the Recovery Act and provide another opportunity to discuss emerging issues and challenges. In addition, several Intergovernmental Audit Forum meetings were scheduled at the regional level across the country and sought to do the same. This regional coordination and information sharing directly contributed to our Recovery Act work in the states. For example, our western regional director made a presentation at the Pacific Northwest Audit Forum regarding our efforts to coordinate with state and local officials in conducting Recovery Act oversight. In conjunction with that forum and at other related forums, she regularly met with the principals of state and local audit entities to coordinate oversight of Recovery Act spending.

Officials from New York City also played a role in creating networks to share information. Believing that large cities were probably facing similar issues and challenges, Recovery officials in New York City established the American Recovery and Reinvestment Act Big City Network (BCN) to serve as a peer exchange group and facilitate information sharing among large municipalities across the country. The group was composed of over 20 large cities with geographical diversity, such as Los Angeles, Philadelphia, Phoenix, and Seattle, that received a significant amount of federal stimulus funding. The former head of the BCN told us that the organization held frequent teleconferences and used this collaboration to elevate issues unique to large cities with OMB, the White House's Recovery Implementation Office, and the Recovery Board. For example, BCN informally surveyed its members in January 2010 concerning each grant and associated funds they received. From this survey, BCN officials assembled a list of cross-jurisdictional issues reflecting the perspectives and experiences of large cities and shared them with the White House, OMB, and the Recovery Board. Likewise, OMB, the Recovery Implementation Office, and the Recovery Board used BCN as a vehicle for getting information out to its partners on the ground.

Similarly, at the state level, a network was established where state Recovery Act coordinators shared information and lessons learned on a weekly basis. This state-level network also discussed ongoing Recovery Act policy and operational issues with the White House, OMB, and the Recovery Board to ensure successful implementation. Federal officials joined the state calls on a regular basis. Both BCN and the state network proved to be especially helpful in fostering intergovernmental communications. For example, the former head of the BCN stated that in response to a Senate Committee request in 2012, New York City leveraged both BCN and the state Recovery Act coordinators' network to inform the current discussion on the Digital Accountability and Transparency Act, proposed legislation which seeks to improve grant transparency through increased reporting.[26] Cities and states mobilized quickly and came together on key consensus principles for Congress' consideration.

Organizations Worked Together in New Ways to Achieve Common Goals

Under the tight time frames set for implementation of the Recovery Act, federal agencies needed to work together to accomplish their goals. For example, HUD and DOE shared a goal of weatherizing low-income households through long-term energy efficiency improvements. To get the projects under way as quickly as possible, they worked together to ensure that homeowners met income standards. Before Recovery Act implementation, both DOE and HUD conducted their own independent income verifications. In May of 2009, DOE and HUD entered into a memorandum of understanding that eliminated the need for separate DOE income verification for people whose incomes had already been verified by HUD. According to DOE officials, this collaboration helped projects move faster, reduced the cost and administrative burden of duplicative verifications, and helped DOE weatherize numerous homes under the Recovery Act through 2013. DOE officials reported that between fiscal years 2010 and 2013, the joint effort helped weatherize approximately 1.7 million housing units, the majority of which were low-income. This policy of sharing low-income verifications for weatherizing homes has continued post-Recovery Act.

At the state level, Massachusetts is an example where officials developed new ways of working together to achieve Recovery Act goals. For example, Massachusetts state officials established the Stimulus Oversight and Prevention (STOP) Fraud Task Force in 2009 to fulfill the Recovery Act's goal of preventing fraud, waste, and abuse of Recovery Act funds. This task force included the state OIG's office, the Attorney General's office, and the State Auditor. Over the next 2 years, the group met bimonthly to discuss fraud prevention and collaborated with several federal agencies including the Department of Justice, the Federal Bureau of Investigation, and HUD. The group also brought in federal OIGs including DOE and Education, the state Comptroller's office, and the Massachusetts Recovery and Reinvestment Office to discuss our report findings and OMB guidance. According to officials from the Massachusetts Attorney General's office, the task force improved communication and furthered efforts to avoid overlap.

The Recovery Act Prompted Adjustments and Innovations in Oversight to Foster Accountability

Faced with the short time frames and accelerated roll out of Recovery Act funds, both the oversight community and agencies adjusted their oversight approach and innovated to foster accountability for Recovery Act funds at the federal and state agency levels. These organizations became more engaged in up-front analysis and monitoring of programs under the Recovery Act and their reviews were often issued before money was spent. These practices included (1) assessing and planning for risks up front; (2) reviewing programs before and while they were being funded rather than waiting until after programs were implemented; (3) communicating findings quickly through informal processes as opposed to regular full reports; and (4) using advanced data analytics.

Increased Use of up-Front Risk Assessments and Planning

At the federal level, several agency OIGs conducted up-front risk planning to proactively prepare for the influx of Recovery Act funds. For example, the Department of Transportation's (DOT) OIG instituted a three-phase risk assessment process for DOT programs that received Recovery Act funds. The

OIG first identified existing program risks based on past reports; it next assessed what the department was doing to address those risks; and it then conducted the audit work. DOT's OIG is continuing to use this three-phase scan approach for its work on Hurricane Sandy.

At the Department of Education, when the OIG realized that Education's discretionary grant budget would increase from a typical allotment of $60 billion annually to over $100 billion under the Recovery Act, officials put aside their initial work plan and developed a new one which focused on the Recovery Act. Toward this end, the OIG conducted up-front risk assessments by looking at its prior work to identify persistent implementation issues going back to fiscal year 2003. The OIG then issued a 2009 capping report that summarized these issues. This report and additional risk assessments on Recovery Act-specific issues guided the OIG's internal control audits that focused on the use of funds, cash management, subrecipient monitoring, and data quality for Recovery Act education programs.

Shortly after the Recovery Act was signed, DOE's OIG reviewed the challenges the agency would need to address to effectively manage the unprecedented level of funding and to meet the goals of the Recovery Act. The resulting report was based on a body of work by the OIG to improve operations and management practices.[27] The OIG identified specific risks that they discovered during past reviews and investigations. The OIG also suggested actions that should be considered during Recovery Act planning and program execution to help reduce the likelihood that these historical problems would recur. Further, the OIG described the department's initial efforts to identify risks and to develop strategies to satisfy the Recovery Act's goals and objectives. In addition, the report outlined the OIG's planned oversight approach which adopted a risk-based strategy that included, among other things, early evaluations of internal controls and assessments of performance outcomes.

At HUD, regional offices conducted front-end risk assessments of programs that would be receiving Recovery Act funds. The HUD OIG considered these risk assessments when preparing its work plan and carrying out audits. The office also conducted capacity reviews for programs that field offices had identified as having known issues. The purpose of these capacity reviews was to enable the office to actively address and work to resolve known issues before Recovery Act funds were distributed to programs.

At the state level, audit organizations also adjusted their usual approaches when planning and conducting reviews of grant programs that received Recovery Act funds. Several state auditors conducted extra audit work of state programs up front in an effort to identify risks and inform their work moving forward. For example, the Office of the California State Auditor conducted "readiness reviews" that highlighted known vulnerabilities in programs receiving Recovery Act money. The office used the information coming out of these reviews to identify specific issues to focus on in future work as well as to inform the oversight committees of the state legislature and other state officials involved in Recovery Act oversight and implementation. As a result of one such review that focused on DOE's Weatherization Assistance Program, the State Auditor was able to identify key implementation issues that needed attention at a joint meeting of state and federal officials organized by the Governor's Recovery Act Task Force. The readiness review identified specific areas where the program needed to improve and informed the frequency with which state auditors would go back to program officials to check on progress. According to the California state auditor, among the benefits of this approach was the feedback it provided to state agencies on their level of readiness as well as the detailed information given to both the state legislature and the Governor's Recovery Act Task Force on the agency's progress. The use of readiness reviews has continued post-Recovery Act. Most recently, the office employed the approach in 2013 as it prepared to audit the implementation of the Affordable Care Act in California.

Increased Use of "Real Time" Information

The Recovery Act's short time frames prompted the oversight community to carry out some of its reviews in "real time" as Recovery funds were being rolled out, as opposed to the traditional approach of reviewing a program after implementation. Under this approach, members of the oversight community looked for ways to inform program officials of challenges and needed improvements much earlier in the process. For example, as described previously in table 1, the Recovery Act specified several roles for us, including conducting bimonthly reviews of selected states' and localities' use of funds made available under the Act. We subsequently selected a core group of 16 states and the District of Columbia to follow over the next few years to provide an ongoing longitudinal analysis of the use of funds provided in conjunction with the Recovery Act. The Recovery Act also assigned us a range of responsibilities to help promote accountability and transparency. Some were recurring requirements such as providing bimonthly reviews of the use of funds made available under various provisions of the Recovery Act by selected states and localities and reviews of quarterly reports on job creation and job retention as reported by Recovery Act fund recipients. Other requirements included targeted studies in several areas such as small business lending, education, and trade adjustment assistance. In total, we issued approximately 125 reports on, or related to, the Recovery Act resulting in more than 65 documented accomplishments.

The interest in obtaining "real time" feedback concerning Recovery Act implementation was not limited to the oversight community. For example, DOT's Federal Highway Administration (FHWA) established National Review Teams (NRT) within 3 months of the Recovery Act's passage to help assist its division offices attain the greater level of accountability and transparency called for under the Recovery Act. As we previously reported, the NRTs were composed of FHWA staff—separated from the rest of FHWA—to act as a neutral third party to conduct oversight.[28] The mission of the NRTs was to conduct quick reviews of FHWA programs and assess processes and compliance with federal requirements in six key risk areas: (1) preliminary plans, specifications, and estimates; (2) contract administration; (3) quality assurance of construction materials; (4) local public agencies; (5) disadvantaged business enterprises; and (6) eligibility for payments. As a review progressed, the NRT discussed findings with division office and state transportation staff. According to FHWA officials, independent reviews had several benefits:

- a consistent, comparative perspective on the oversight regularly conducted by division offices, and the collection of information at the national level on both best practices and recurring trouble spots across FHWA division offices;
- additional "boots on the ground" for project-level oversight and increased awareness of federal oversight activity among states, Metropolitan Planning Organizations, and other transportation organizations receiving Recovery Act funds; and
- an independent outside voice to examine Recovery Act projects and point out problems, keeping the partnering relationship between the division offices and the state DOTs intact.

Division offices and state officials with whom we spoke responded positively to the NRT reviews. The NRT was viewed as a success for FHWA and it has since added independent reviews based largely on the NRT model to provide independent corporate level review of projects and programs in addition to providing other support services.

Earlier Communication of Audit Findings

The rapid pace at which Recovery Act funds were being distributed also prompted audit organizations to communicate their findings earlier in the audit process. For example, DOT's OIG issued periodic advisories within the agency rather than waiting until an audit was completed to share its findings. According to OIG staff, these advisories informed the department of issues or concerns shortly after they were discovered, thereby permitting program staff to take corrective action much more quickly.

In our first report on our bimonthly reviews of the use of Recovery Act funds by selected states and localities, we determined that the Single Audit process needed adjustment to provide the necessary level of focus and accountability over Recovery Act funds in a timelier manner than the current schedule.[29] Subsequently, we recommended that the director of OMB adjust the Single Audit process to provide for review of the design of internal controls during 2009 over programs to receive Recovery Act funding, before significant expenditures in 2010. In response, in October 2009 OMB implemented the Single Audit Internal Control Project—a collaborative effort between 16 volunteer states receiving Recovery Act funds, their auditors, and the federal government—to achieve more timely communication of internal control deficiencies for higher-risk Recovery Act programs.[30] The project encouraged auditors to identify and communicate significant deficiencies and material weaknesses in internal controls over compliance for selected major Recovery Act programs 3 months sooner than the 9-month time frame required under statute. The project allowed program management officials at an audited agency to expedite corrective action and help mitigate the risk of improper Recovery Act expenditures. In May 2010, we reported that the project met some of its objectives and was helpful in identifying critical areas where further OMB actions were needed to improve the Single Audit process over Recovery Act funding.[31]

Auditors at the local level also communicated their findings early. For example, the Denver City Auditor's Office adopted new practices to provide more timely information on Recovery Act programs to the Mayor and other key officials, particularly on issues affecting compliance with Recovery Act reporting requirements. Using a tiered notification process, the auditor's office would initially notify the appropriate city department informally through e-mail or a similar means of potential issues they were finding during an on-going audit. The auditor's office would revisit the issues later and, if the office determined the issue had not been addressed, it would then formally communicate any substantive issue on a real-time basis through an "audit alert." These alerts were typically brief documents and went to the affected departments as well as directly to the Mayor's work group that oversaw the city's Recovery Act implementation. If appropriate action was still not forthcoming, the city auditor might issue a public alert or maybe a full public audit report. According to a senior city audit official, the alerts were beneficial because the city auditor did not have to conduct a full audit to communicate risks and findings to decision makers, allowing them to more quickly address problems. The city auditor issued its first audit alert in October 2009 and subsequently issued another one in February 2010 when problems from the first one had not been addressed. After the second alert, the city administration corrected the identified problems.

Use of Advanced Data Analytics

To further increase accountability under the Recovery Act, the Recovery Board utilized innovative data analytics in carrying out its oversight responsibilities. Data analytics is a term typically used to describe a variety of techniques that can be used to analyze and interpret data to, among other things, help identify and reduce fraud, waste, and abuse. Specifically, predictive analytic technologies can be used to identify potential fraud and errors before payments are made, while other techniques, such as data-mining and data-matching of multiple databases, can identify fraud or improper payments that have already been awarded, thus assisting agencies in recovering these dollars.[32] In October 2009, the Recovery Board established an innovative center to analyze the use of Recovery Act funds by employing data analytics (see figure 3). The Recovery Operations Center (ROC) served as a centralized location for analyzing Recovery Act funds and their recipients through the use of such predictive analytic technologies.

According to Recovery Board staff, the results of these approaches provided the OIG community and other oversight authorities with information they could use to focus limited resources on cities, regions, and high-risk government programs where historical data and current trends suggested the likelihood of future risk. ROC analysts would cross-reference lists of grant recipients or sub-recipients against a variety of databases to look for risk indicators such as criminal convictions, lawsuits, tax liens, bankruptcies, risky financial deals, or suspension/debarment proceedings.

One tool used to do this is link analysis, which assists the analyst in making connections by visually representing investigative findings. Link analysis charts visually depict how individuals and companies are connected, what awards an entity has received, and how these actors may be linked to any derogatory information obtained from the databases described above . Such tools, when combined with enhanced Geographic Information System capabilities, enable ROC analysts to conduct geospatial analysis by displaying data from multiple datasets on maps to help them make linkages and discover potential problems.

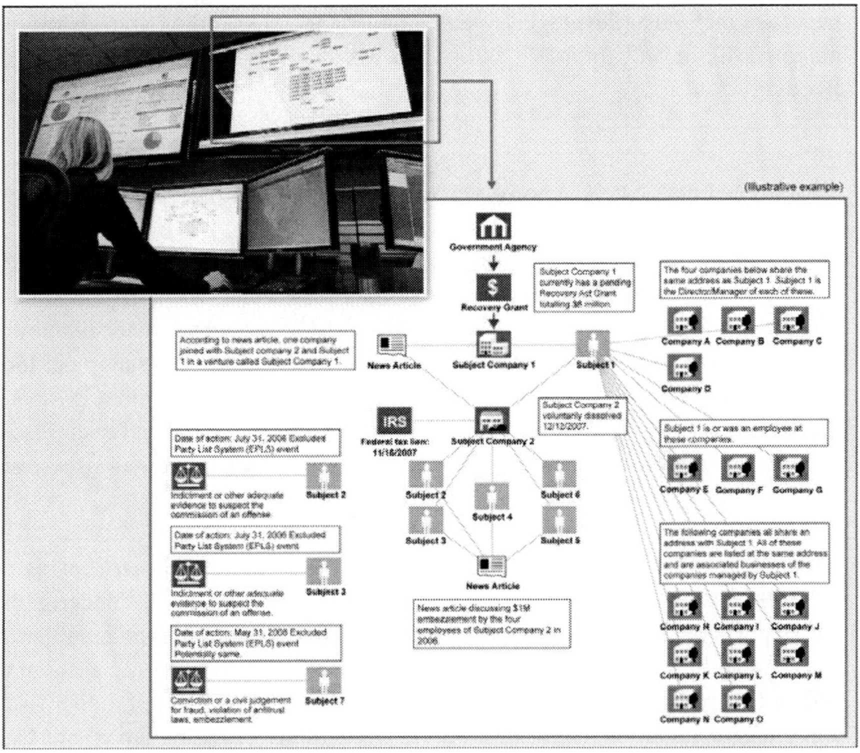

Source: GAO representation of Recovery Board information; Recovery Board (photo).

Figure 3. An Analyst Working in the Recovery Board's Recovery Operations Center and a Sample Output of One of ROC's Link Analysis Tools.

For example, the ROC helped a federal agency investigate possible contract fraud related to over-billing on multiple contracts. ROC analysts found 99 recipient awards made to a single company totaling over $12 million. In another example, the ROC helped to investigate allegations of false claims and major fraud against the United States. ROC analysts found officers of one company were also executives of more than 15 other companies, many of which were located at the same address, and collectively received millions in Recovery Act funds.

More recently, the ROC has been used to track funds and help reduce fraud, waste, and abuse related to the tens of billions of dollars that have been awarded to states and communities to assist in their recovery after Hurricane Sandy hit in October 2012. Recovery Board staff have sought to leverage the expertise they have developed in analyzing financial spending and identifying potential fraud and high-risk indicators based on their experience with the Recovery Act.

The Recovery Act's Accountability Requirements Also Presented Oversight Challenges

To assure the public that their tax dollars were being spent efficiently and effectively, the Recovery Act called for increased oversight and accountability of those funds by oversight and program entities at the federal, state, and local levels. This increased emphasis on oversight and accountability presented challenges for those entities stemming from (1) a lack of financial resources to conduct oversight at the state and local levels, (2) human capital issues, and (3) the accelerated roll out of Recovery Act funds.

Limited Resources to Conduct Oversight at the State and Local Levels

Officials with whom we spoke in several states expressed concerns that the Recovery Act did not provide funding to state oversight entities, although it placed additional federal requirements on them to provide proper accounting and to ensure transparency. Federal agency OIG offices received a significant amount to conduct oversight of Recovery Act funds—ranging anywhere from $1 million to $48.25 million distributed to more than 28 agencies. In contrast, states and localities relied on their existing budgets and human capital resources (and, in some cases, supplemented by a small percentage of administrative funds) to carry out their additional oversight activities.

Due to fiscal constraints, states reported significant declines in the number of management and oversight staff—limiting states' ability to ensure proper implementation and management of Recovery Act funds. With oversight capacity already strained in many states, the situation was further exacerbated by increased workloads resulting from implementation of new or expanded grant programs funded by the Recovery Act. For example, Massachusetts officials explained that the state oversight community faced budget cuts of about 10 percent. According to officials from the OIG and the State Auditor's office, their budgets are almost entirely composed of salaries, and any cuts in funding resulted in fewer staff available to conduct oversight. As a result of the cuts, the Inspector General stated that his department did not have the resources to conduct any additional oversight related to Recovery Act funds. Further, the Massachusetts State Auditor described how his department had to furlough staff for 6 days in fiscal year 2009. In recognition of this situation and reflective of the state's desire to pursue fraud in the Recovery Act program, for state fiscal years 2009 through 2012, the Massachusetts Recovery and Reinvestment Office allocated funds from the state's central administration account to the Attorney General, State Auditor, and OIG offices to ensure that oversight would take place.

The California State Auditor also cited the lack of federal funding for state and local oversight as a challenge to ensuring accountability in the implementation of the Recovery Act. In a 2009 testimony to the California state budget committee, the State Auditor said that her office would need to conduct an additional 14 audits based on an initial analysis of the estimated stimulus funds that California would receive. Furthermore, the programs that the office was auditing at the time received additional funds, which potentially increased the workload and cost to audit those programs as well. Finally, new requirements created by the Recovery Act for existing programs also impacted the State Audit Office's efforts. The California State Auditor noted that given the additional responsibilities her office faced due to the influx of stimulus funds, any budget cuts would adversely affect the office's ability to conduct audits.

In another example, Colorado's state auditor reported that state oversight capacity was limited during Recovery Act implementation, noting that the Department of Health Care Policy and Financing had three controllers in 4 years and the state legislature's Joint Budget Committee cut field audit staff for the Department of Human Services in half. In addition, the Colorado DOT's deputy controller position was vacant, as was the Department of Personnel & Administration's internal auditor position. Colorado officials noted that these actions were, in part, due to administrative cuts during a past economic downturn in an attempt to maintain program delivery levels.

Accelerated Rollout of Recovery Act Programs Presented Oversight Challenges

The President's goal for quickly spending Recovery Act funds created a large spike in spending for a number of programs in the 28 agencies receiving

Recovery Act funds. The act also created a number of new programs—requiring agencies to move quickly. As a result, under the Recovery Act's accelerated rollout requirements, some federal agencies and states faced oversight challenges.

For example, DOT and states faced numerous challenges in implementing the Recovery Act's maintenance-of-effort oversight mechanism due to the accelerated rollout of funds. The Recovery Act contains maintenance of effort provisions designed to prevent recipients, such as state DOTs, public housing agencies, and private companies, from substituting planned spending for a given program with Recovery Act funds. That is, the provisions ensured that the increased federal spending would supplement rather than replace state, local, or private spending.[33] The maintenance-of-effort provision for DOT in the Recovery Act required the governor of each state to certify that the state would maintain its planned level of transportation spending from February 17, 2009, through September 30, 2010.[34] Twenty-one states did not meet their certified planned spending levels, and a January 2011 preliminary DOT report found that some of these states were unclear on what constituted "state funding". DOT also found some of the states were unclear about how well DOT guidance on calculating planned expenditures would work in the many different contexts in which it would have to operate. As a result, many problems came to light only after DOT had issued initial guidance and states had submitted their first certifications. DOT issued guidance seven times during the first year after the act was signed to clarify how states were to calculate their planned or actual expenditures for their maintenance-of-effort certifications. Further, many states did not have an existing means to identify planned transportation expenditures for a specific period, and their financial and accounting systems did not capture that data. Therefore, according to DOT and some state officials, a more narrowly focused requirement applying only to programs administered by state DOTs or to programs that typically receive state funding could have helped address the maintenance-of-effort challenges. DOT and state officials told us that while the maintenance-of-effort requirement can be useful for ensuring continued investment in transportation, allowing more flexibility for differences in states and programs, and adjustments for unexpected changes to states' economic conditions, should be considered for future provisions.

At DOE, the department initially encountered some challenges with fully developing a management and accountability infrastructure because of the large amount of Recovery Act funding it received in a short period of time. According to an official in the DOE OIG's office, this was especially true with the new Energy Efficiency Conservation Block Grant program.[35] This official told us that some states and localities also did not have the infrastructure in place (including the necessary training) to manage the large amount of additional federal funding. Further, DOE required recipients' weatherization plans to address how the respective state's current and expanded workforce (employees and contractors) would be trained. In May 2010, according to DOE, the agency was in the process of developing national standards for weatherization certification and accreditation. DOE estimated that developing the standards would take about 2 years—a time frame that did not match the accelerated timing of the Recovery Act's funds' distribution. Several years after the Recovery Act was implemented, DOE reported that it had completed certain milestones toward developing national standards for weatherization, training, certification, and accreditation, but was still working to finalize other elements such as its national certification program.

THE RECOVERY ACT RESULTED IN INCREASED TRANSPARENCY BUT ALSO PRESENTED CHALLENGES

Recovery Act Transparency Websites Embody Several Leading Practices

In an April 2009 memorandum, OMB directed agencies to follow leading practices for federal website development and management, such as those listed on HowTo.gov, a website managed by the Federal Web Managers Council and the General Services Administration.[36] HowTo.gov makes available a list of the "Top 10 Best Practices" for federal websites as a resource to improve how agencies communicate and interact with customers and provide services.[37] Recovery.gov, as well as selected state and city Recovery websites, demonstrated several of these leading practices including establishing a clear purpose of the website, using social networking tools to garner interest in the website, tailoring websites to meet audience needs, and obtaining stakeholder input when designing the website. In addition, we found that some websites enabled place-based performance reporting.

Establish a Clear Purpose of the Website

Consistent with leading practices for the development of federal websites on HowTo.gov, Recovery.gov and selected state Recovery websites clearly identify for the user the purposes of the site and the ways it can be used to accomplish tasks efficiently. According to HowTo.gov, this is important because people often visit government websites with a specific task in mind, and if it is not easy to find the information quickly that they need to complete that task, they will leave the site. Recovery.gov contains an entire page that outlines what users can do on the site, including how to use the raw data available through the website; report waste, fraud, and abuse; or find job and grant opportunities. Further, Recovery.gov has a "Get Started" page with an overview of the information on the site including Recovery Act goals, the Recovery Board's mission, what information is not available on the website, and what users can do on the website.

Similarly, Massachusetts' Recovery website has tabs on its homepage that link to information on how to use the website to track Recovery Act jobs, spending, vendors, and the impact of Recovery Act dollars in the state.[38] For example, the "track jobs" page informs users how they can track jobs created and retained in their community and provides a user guide to assist them in their query.

Use Social Networking Tools to Garner Interest in the Website

Another leading practice for federal websites includes the use of social networking tools. According to Howto.gov, social media is transforming how government engages with citizens, allowing agencies to share information and deliver services more quickly and effectively than ever before. Recovery.gov and selected state and local Recovery websites use social networking tools to garner interest in their websites. These websites integrated Web 2.0 technologies to help people share and use the information they provide. For example, to develop web-based communities of interest, Recovery.gov has a dedicated social media web page that has links to Recovery's presence on various social-networking tools such as Facebook, Twitter, YouTube, and Flickr.[39] Recovery.gov's social media page enables users to (1) download a Recovery application for iPhones and for iPads with a mapping feature showing how Recovery Act funds were being spent, (2) sign up for a Recovery.gov month-inreview email, and (3) sign up to receive Recovery RSS web feeds.[40] Finally, Recovery.gov also has a blog, written by Recovery Board staff, with a stated purpose to further a dialogue on transparency and accountability in government, as well as to provide a forum for thoughts, comments, and suggestions from the public.

New York City also made use of social networking to communicate information regarding Recovery Act implementation through the use of a

Tumblr blog. [41] City officials used this blog to communicate stories and examples to its residents about how it was using Recovery Act funds and the impact of those investments.[42] City officials said the blog allowed them to get behind full-time equivalent numbers and dollar expenditures so that people could better understand how the Recovery Act was helping them tackle problems where they work and live. For example, the blog described one project that had no net increase in jobs but still made a valuable difference for the city because Recovery Act funds were used to repair 300,000 potholes and move to zero diesel fuel emissions for city vehicles.

Tailor Website to Meet Audience Needs

Organizing a website according to the needs of its audience is also a key leading practice for federal websites since an agency's goal is to build the right website for the people who need it and serve them effectively by learning as much as possible about the website's customers and what they do. Recovery.gov has dedicated pages for different audiences that compile and organize relevant resources according to their needs and interests. On its home page, Recovery.gov has a tab which provides links to pages designed with specific users in mind such as citizens, the press, and grant recipients. There are also links to pages on neighborhood Recovery Act projects, information on the Recovery Board, and other information users are looking for. For example, grant recipients have a dedicated page that provides resources such as reporting timelines, user guides, a service/help desk, recipient reporting information, and a recipient awards map. (See figure 4.)

On Recovery.gov's "Developer Center" web page, users can access data reported by recipients of Recovery awards through the Recovery application program interface (API) and the Mapping API.[43] Users can also find widgets providing data summaries by state, county, congressional district, or ZIP code as reported by recipients.[44] The web page also has a tool for users to build customized charts and graphs displaying information such as funds awarded and received by state, agencies by number of awards, and spending categories by funds awarded.

The state of Massachusetts also tailored its Recovery Act website to meet its audience's needs. Prior to its implementation of the Recovery Act's transparency provisions, Massachusetts had little experience with electronic reporting and disclosure of federal contracts, grants, and loans. The MassRecovery website provided weekly citizen updates and testimonials of how spending has benefited lives. The Citizens' Update web page provides a summary of where the state's Recovery Act dollars are going, where jobs are being created and retained, and information on beneficiaries of funds received. In December 2009, MASSPIRG, an independent consumer research group, issued a brief pointing to the strengths of the Massachusetts Recovery website including the ability of the Citizens' Update web page to show money spent and jobs created and retained in easy-to-read pie charts and tables; a summary of funds distributed through the state; and an interactive state map of Recovery Act spending. Further, in January 2010, Good Jobs First, a national policy resource center, reviewed and evaluated states' Recovery Act websites. The organization ranked Massachusetts' Recovery website on its top 10 list citing such beneficial features as the site's comprehensive search engine, data download capability, and information on five key Recovery Act project elements—description, dollar amount, recipient name, status, and the text of the award.

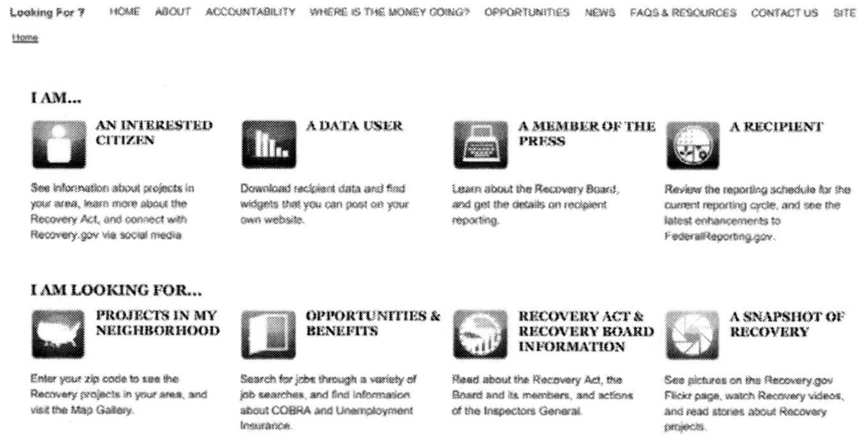

Source: Recovery.gov.

Note: The link to the above web page is http://www.recovery.gov/arra /Pages/audience_landing.aspx

Figure 4. Screenshot of Recovery.gov User Identification Feature.

Obtain Stakeholder Input When Designing the Website

Leading website practices also recommend that developers obtain stakeholder input when designing federal websites by engaging potential users through focus groups and other outreach; regularly conducting usability tests to gather insight into navigation, the organization of content, and the ease with which different types of users can complete specific tasks; and collecting and analyzing performance, customer satisfaction, and other metrics. According to leading website practices, these efforts are important for collecting and analyzing information about audiences, their needs, and how they are using, or want to use, the website.

The developers of Recovery.gov followed this leading practice by using input from user forums, focus groups, and usability testing with interested citizens to collect feedback and recommendations, which then inform the development of the website from its initial stages. For example, teaming with OMB and the National Academy of Public Administration, the developers of Recovery.gov hosted a week-long electronic town hall meeting at the end of April 2009 entitled "Recovery Dialogue on Information Technology Solutions." Over 500 citizens, information technology specialists, and website development experts registered for the event and submitted numerous ideas. Recovery.gov adopted some of the ideas right away and included others in the re-launched version of the website in September 2009. These changes included a standardized reporting system for recipients, a greater use of maps, and a feedback section for users. Additionally, in October 2009, Recovery.gov developers conducted remote usability testing with 72 users, where the developers received suggested changes, some of which they later implemented. Further, in 2012, significant changes were made to Recovery.gov based on user feedback on the website. These changes included creating a recipient and agency data page, agency profiles, and a new Recipient Projects Map with a series of dropdown menus and checkboxes that enable users to filter data so they can see it in a targeted fashion (for example, by state, agency, or category).

Enable Place-Based Performance Reporting

For websites covering numerous projects at various locations, a place-based geographic information system can be a useful tool. According to the White House's Digital Government Strategy, the federal government needs to be customer-centric when designing digital service platforms such as websites. In other words, agencies need to be responsive to customers' needs by making it easy to find and share electronic information and accomplish important tasks. From the beginning, recipient reported data on Recovery.gov was geo-coded in a way that made it possible for users to find awards and track the progress of projects on a block-by-block basis. The presentation of information on Recovery.gov and on many state websites generally targeted individual citizens who were not experts in data analysis. The format and content of data prioritized mapping capabilities and invited people to enter their ZIP code and locate projects in their immediate area.

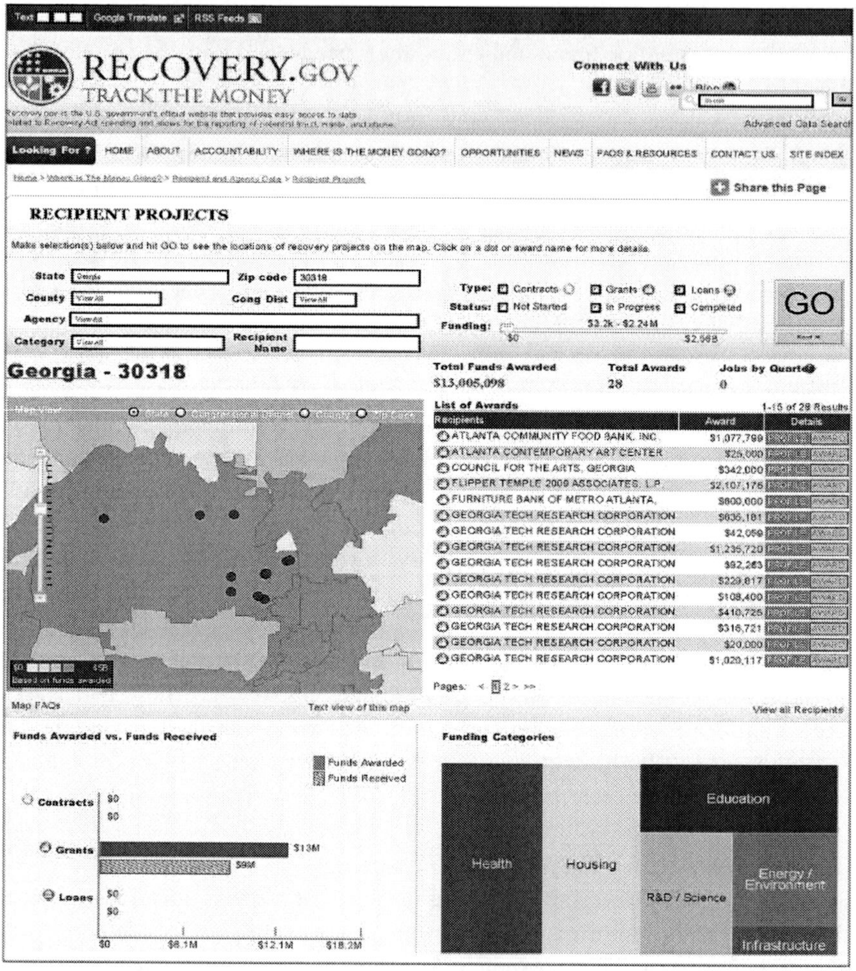

Source: Recovery.gov.

Note: The link to access Recovery.gov's recipient projects page can be found at http://www.recovery.gov/arra/Transparency/RecoveryData/Pages/RecipientReportedD ata Map.aspx

Figure 5. Screenshot of Recovery.gov's Recipient Projects Page for a Georgia ZIP Code, 30318.

For example, figure 5 shows the map a user sees if ZIP code 30318 in Georgia is entered into this web page. From this map, the user can click on any of the dots that represent Recovery projects to find out information such as the project recipient name, award amount, project description, number of jobs created, and completion status. Additional information available to users includes the amount of funds received by recipients as well as the overall distribution of grants by funding categories for that area.

States and localities also utilized mapping features on their Recovery websites. For example, in New York City, Recovery officials launched a Recovery Act website, the NYCStat Stimulus Tracker, as an interactive, comprehensive reporting tool. The federal government's website, Recovery.gov, served as the design inspiration and, according to a senior city official, Stimulus Tracker was one of the first publicly-accessible websites to report Recovery Act data for a local jurisdiction. City Recovery officials were able to develop and launch New York City's stimulus website more quickly than other locations—approximately 6 weeks from start to completion—because they were able to leverage a previously implemented information technology platform to support citywide performance reporting. Stimulus Tracker allowed the public to explore several levels deeper than what was at Recovery.gov, which reported at the funding award level. For example, Stimulus Tracker broke down each award into several projects, each of which had its own dashboard page that displayed information such as (1) the status of the project, (2) the percentage of total funds spent, (3) start date and spending deadlines, and (4) the number of jobs created or retained. Visitors to the site could drill into a record of every payment made with stimulus funds through the additional feature "Payment Tracker" and every contract to carry out stimulus-funded work through "Contract Tracker."

Stimulus Tracker also offered an interactive map for site visitors who were interested in knowing how stimulus dollars were allocated geographically and where specific projects were located. This information was layered on top of the city's existing online map portal. It included such items as the locations of schools, libraries, hospitals, and subways, as well as online property, building, statistics, and census information. As New York City's existing online map portal could already be navigated either by entering a specific address or simply using zoom and scroll tools, city Recovery Act officials were able to build on this application and include a city mapping tool for Recovery Act funds where the public could find any project with a discrete location. See figure 6 for a screen shot of New York City's mapping tool depicting the city's Recovery Act projects.

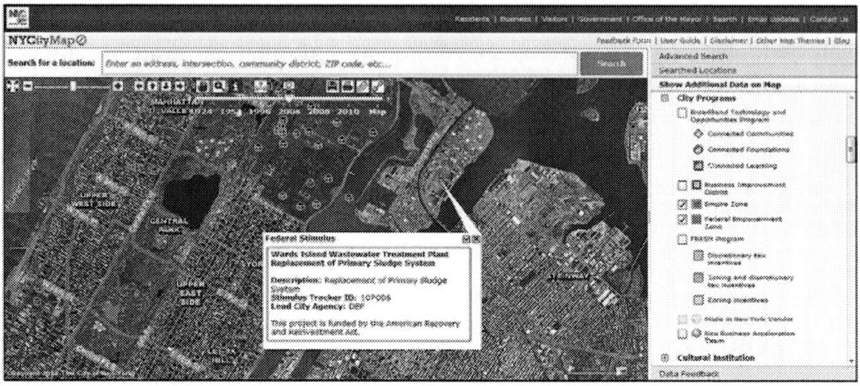

Source: City of New York (Copyright © 2013, The City of New York).
Note: The link to the NYC Stimulus Tracker webpage is http://maps.nyc.gov/doitt/nycitymap/?featuretypes=STIMULUS

Figure 6. Screenshot of NYCStat Stimulus Tracker Mapping Feature.

Recovery Act Performance Was Mostly Measured by Outputs Rather than Outcomes, and Challenges with Both Existed

Recipients and Agencies Were Required to Report Amount and Speed of Funding but Faced Challenges in Doing So

The Recovery Act requires recipients to report on their use of funding and agencies that provide those funds to make the reports publicly available.[45] The Recovery Act's recipient reporting requirements apply only to nonfederal recipients of funding, including all entities other than individuals receiving Recovery Act funds directly from the federal government such as state and local governments, private companies, educational institutions, nonprofits, and other private organizations. As required by section 1512(c) of the Recovery Act, recipients were to submit quarterly reports that included the total amount of Recovery Act funds received, the amount of funds expended or obligated to projects or activities, and a detailed list of those projects or activities.[46] For each project or activity, the detailed list was to include the project's name, description, and an evaluation of its completion status. Also, the recipient reports were to include detailed information on any subcontracts or subgrants as required by the Federal Funding Accountability and Transparency Act of 2006.[47] For example, recipient reports are required to also include details on sub-awards and other payments.

With the Recovery Act's enhanced reporting requirements on spending, agencies and recipients faced several challenges. Many agencies and state and local partners were limited in their capacity to meet the enhanced reporting requirements due to a lack of knowledge and expertise. Others struggled with the burden of double reporting when they had to report to federal systems tracking Recovery dollars as well as to agency systems because, in some cases, agencies required more data to manage their programs. Finally, some had trouble reporting data for certain projects within the operational limitations of place-based data mapping systems.

Capacity to Meet Reporting Requirements

Many state and local partners were limited in their capacity to meet spending reporting requirements because they lacked knowledge and expertise. Using a centralized mechanism like FederalReporting.gov to capture recipient reporting information was a new process that recipients and agencies had to learn. We have previously reported on the questions raised by state officials regarding the reporting capacities of some local organizations, particularly small rural entities, boards, or commissions, and private entities not used to doing business with the federal government.[48] In addition, some state officials said that the Recovery Act's requirement that recipients report on the use of funds within 10 days after a quarter ends was a challenge because some sub-recipients were unable to send them the needed data on time.

Officials at several agencies suggested that if FederalReporting.gov had allowed certain key award and identifying data fields to be pre-populated each quarter, it would have likely resulted in fewer data errors for agencies to address and eased the reporting burden on recipients. In our September 2013 report and testimony on federal data transparency, we concluded that the transparency envisioned under the Recovery Act for tracking spending was unprecedented for the federal government, requiring the development of a system that could track billions of dollars disbursed to thousands of recipients. Such a system needed to be operational quickly to enable posting of spending information rapidly for a variety of programs. However, because agency systems did not collect spending data in a consistent manner, the most expedient approach for Recovery Act reporting was to collect data directly from fund recipients.[49] Recipients had the additional burden of having to provide this information and when the data had to be entered manually, it could impact the accuracy of the data.[50] Thus, in September 2013 we recommended that the director of OMB, in collaboration with members of the

Government Accountability and Transparency Board, develop a plan to implement comprehensive transparency reform, including a long-term timeline and requirements for data standards, such as establishing a uniform award identification system across the federal government.[51]

Earlier this year, the Recovery Board noted that agencies and OIGs also experienced difficulties adapting to the more frequent reporting (every quarter) and more detailed reporting (e.g., jobs created or individual project activities) required of most government grant recipients.[52] Agency officials acknowledged spending considerable staff hours training recipients, providing technical assistance to them, verifying and validating their data, and following up with them when issues arose. Despite efforts to streamline and enhance existing review protocols, agencies still needed skilled people to review and process applications for awards. Although agencies and OIGs credited outreach to recipients for reducing noncompliance with reporting requirements, the amount of staffing resources it took to conduct that outreach was significant.

Double Reporting

We have previously noted that recipients of Recovery Act funds were required to report similar information to both agency reporting systems and FederalReporting.gov.[53] Several federal agency and state government officials we spoke with also mentioned that reporting to FederalReporting.gov resulted in double reporting for their agency and grantees as several of them deemed their existing internal systems superior and therefore would end up reporting to both. For example, at HUD, program offices were unable to abandon their established reporting systems because the agency's systems collected data necessary to support HUD's grants management and oversight processes. HUD officials told us that requiring grantees to report using two systems resulted in double reporting of data and proved burdensome to recipients and to HUD staff who spent many hours correcting inaccurate entries.

At DOT, officials preferred using the agency's own data because it was more detailed and was reported monthly—more frequently than the Recovery.gov data. In a focus group involving state transportation officials, several echoed the redundancy of reporting systems. These officials indicated that having to report to three systems—the internal state system, DOT's system, and FederalReporting.gov—increased their agencies' burden. As we reported in our previously mentioned September 2013 report and testimony on federal data transparency efforts, the lack of consistent data and standards and commonality in how data elements are defined places undue burden on federal fund recipients. This can result in them having to report the same information multiple times via disparate reporting platforms. [54] To address this issue, as OMB developed procedures for reporting on the use of federal funds, it directed recipients of covered funds to use a series of standardized data elements. Further, rather than report to multiple government entities, each with its own disparate reporting requirements, all recipients of Recovery Act funds were required to centrally report into the Recovery Board's inbound reporting website, FederalReporting.gov.

Difficulty of Using Place-Based GIS Data for Some Types of Projects

While Recovery.gov enabled users to locate Recovery Act projects on a block-by-block basis, some of the Recovery Act data did not lend itself to the geospatial reporting presentation format on the website. For example, according to Recovery Board officials, the website only allowed one location to be reported per project even though some projects spanned multiple locations. Therefore, if a DOT highway project crossed multiple ZIP codes, only one location of performance could be reported. Further, certain locations were difficult to map such as rural roads, post office boxes, county level data, and consultant contractors who worked out of their homes.

Recipients Were Required to Report Outcome Measure of Jobs Created and Retained but Faced Some Challenges

The other major performance measure required under the Recovery Act focused on the estimate of the number of jobs created or number of jobs retained as a result of funding provided by the act. In addition to the previously described reporting on funds spent and activities, recipients were required in their quarterly reports to estimate the number of jobs created or retained by that project or activity.[55] OMB issued clarifying guidance for recipient reporting in June 2009 and recipients began reporting on jobs starting in October 2009.[56] Among other things, the guidance clarified that recipients of Recovery Act funds were to report only on jobs directly created or retained by Recovery Act-funded projects, activities, and contracts. Recipients were not expected to report on the employment impact on materials suppliers ("indirect" jobs) or on the local community. Recipients had 10 days after the end of each calendar quarter to report. OMB's guidance also provided additional instruction on calculating the number of jobs created or retained by Recovery Act funding on a full-time equivalent (FTE) basis.[57]

Recipients faced several challenges meeting these requirements. They had difficulty accurately defining FTEs, as various recipients interpreted and applied the FTE guidance from OMB differently. Further, many recipients struggled to meet reporting deadlines as they had little time to gather, analyze, and pass on information to the federal government at the end of each fiscal quarter.

Definitional Challenges and Discrepancies in Reporting Ftes

Under OMB guidance, jobs created or retained were to be expressed as FTEs. In our November 2009 report we found that recipients reported data inconsistently even though OMB and federal agencies provided significant guidance and training.[58] Specifically, we found that while FTE calculations should allow for different types of jobs—part time, full time or temporary—to be aggregated, differing interpretations of the FTE guidance compromised the recipients' ability to aggregate the data. For example, in California, two higher education systems calculated FTEs differently. One chose to use a 2-month period as the basis for the FTE performance period. The other chose to use a year as the basis. The result was almost a three-to-one difference in the number of FTEs reported for each university system in the first reporting period. Although the Department of Education provided alternative methods for calculating an FTE, in neither case did the guidance explicitly state the period of performance of the FTE. We recommended that OMB clarify the definition of FTE jobs and encourage federal agencies to provide or improve program-specific guidance for recipients. Further, we recommended that OMB be more explicit that jobs created or retained are to be reported as hours worked and paid for by the Recovery Act. In general, OMB and agencies acted upon our recipient reporting-related recommendations and later reporting periods indicated significant improvements in FTE calculations. OMB's guidance changed the original formula and consequently, agencies had to rush to educate recipients about the changes. Agencies spent extra time and resources that quarter reviewing and validating recipient data to reduce errors. In some cases, agencies communicated daily with recipients via phone or e-mail to ensure their report submissions were accurate.

Capacity of Recipients to Meet Deadlines

The requirement to regularly report on jobs created and retained further strained the capacity of some recipients. Recipients only had 10 days after the end of each fiscal quarter to determine this information and pass it on to the federal government.[59] Some state education officials told us that deadlines for reporting should have been extended by 1 to 2 weeks so they were not rushing to input data. One of these officials said she was directed by other state officials to put in "the best data you have, even if it's not correct...and go back and correct it later." City officials also reported concerns with the quick turn-around time for reporting. For example, one city official stated that, in order to meet reporting deadlines, it was necessary had to enter data manually, which created additional work. The Recovery Board accepted these post-correction actions as it extended the quality assurance period to provide more time for agencies to review reports and recipients to make corrections in FederalReporting.gov. As a result, recipients could change their reports up to about 2 weeks before the start of the next reporting period.

Program Specific Performance Measures Varied by Program and Agency with Some Focusing More on Outputs than Outcomes

The administration required agencies receiving Recovery Act funds to submit performance plans that identified additional measures on a program-by-program basis. Consistent with existing GPRA requirements for agencies to set outcome-oriented performance goals and measures, OMB's initial Recovery Act implementation guidance required federal agencies to ensure that program goals were achieved. OMB required agencies to measure specific program outcomes, supported by corresponding quantifiable output measures, and improved results on broader economic indicators. 60 In responding to this requirement, agencies typically resorted to existing measures in their grant programs' performance plans. This information is reported by agency and by program within each agency, as opposed to government-wide. While Recovery.gov provided a template for facilitating the reporting of this information, the level of detail and specificity of outcomes varied greatly for some of the agencies we reviewed, making it difficult to determine the extent to which some were making progress toward their goals and demonstrating results.

For example, Education's performance plan described the agency's accountability mechanisms, the type and scope of project activities, and specific program performance measures. With the exception of the number of jobs created or retained, Education's plan stated the agency was primarily using existing established agency performance measures that applied to both Recovery and non-Recovery funds. For example to measure the success of one type of education grant fund (specifically, Title I of the Elementary and Secondary Education Act of 1965, as amended) which the Recovery Act made available to local educational agencies, Education used existing agency performance measures, such as the percentage of economically disadvantaged students in grades 3 to 8 scoring at the proficient or advanced levels on state reading and mathematics assessments.

On the other hand, DOT filled out the templates to report on its 12 programs, and its performance measures were generally less specific and outcome oriented. For example, DOT's Capital Assistance for High Speed Rail Corridors and Intercity Passenger Rail Service performance plan metrics included whether interim guidance was published within time frames, the number of applicants received for the program, and the number of grants awarded for the program. Further, as we previously reported, DOT released a series of performance plans in May 2009 to measure the impact of Recovery Act transportation programs, but these plans generally did not contain an extensive discussion of the specific goals and measures to assess the impact of Recovery Act projects.[61] For example, while the plan for the highway program contained a section on anticipated results, three of its five measures were the percent of funds obligated and expended and the number of projects under construction. The fourth measure was the percentage of vehicle miles traveled on pavement on the National Highway System rated in good condition, but the plan said that goals for improvement with Recovery Act funds were yet to be determined. The fifth goal was number of miles of roadway improved, and DOT's plan reported that even with the addition of Recovery Act funds, the new target would remain the same as previously planned. As a result, we recommended in May 2010 that DOT ensure that the results of these projects were assessed and a determination made about whether these investments produced long-term benefits. DOT did not implement our recommendation.

CONCLUDING OBSERVATIONS

Created in response to the recent serious recession, the Recovery Act represents a significant financial investment in improving the economy. Grant programs were a key mechanism for distributing this support. By increasing accountability and transparency requirements while at the same time setting aggressive timelines for the distribution of funds, the Recovery Act created high expectations as well as uncertainty and risk for federal, state, and local governments responsible for implementing the law.

Faced with these challenges, some of these organizations looked beyond their usual way of doing business and adjusted their usual practices to help ensure the accountability and transparency of Recovery Act funds. The oversight community adopted a faster and more flexible approach to how they conducted and reported on their audits and reviews so that their findings could inform programs of needed corrections before all Recovery funds were expended. They leveraged technology by using advanced data analytics to reduce fraud and to create easily accessible Internet resources that greatly improved the public's access to, and ability to make use of, data about grants funded by the Recovery Act. These and other experiences, as well as the challenges identified in this report, provide potentially valuable lessons for the future. Underlying many of these lessons is the importance of increased coordination and collaboration, both vertically—transcending federal, state, and local levels of government—and horizontally—across organizational silos within the federal community—to share information and work towards common goals.

One question that remains unresolved is the extent to which good practices developed in response to the Recovery Act's special challenges and conditions can ultimately be incorporated in everyday practice for managing and overseeing grants. Some of the practices we found, such as the use of the Recovery Operations Center and state readiness reviews, have been able to make this transition. Others, such as some of the information sharing networks established during the Recovery Act, have had more difficulty in doing so. Proposals under consideration by Congress and the administration to extend Recovery Act requirements for spending transparency to all federal grants suggest that this has been the case for tracking dollars.[62] Still to be seen is whether it will be possible to provide this type of government-wide transparency to other measures of performance, such as grant outcomes.

AGENCY COMMENTS

We provided a draft of this report to the Secretaries of the Departments of Education, Energy, Housing and Urban Development, and Transportation; and to the Director of the Office of Management and Budget. We also provided drafts of the examples included in this report to cognizant officials from the relevant state and local agencies to verify accuracy and completeness, and we made technical changes and clarifications where appropriate. The agencies generally agreed with our findings and provided technical comments which were incorporated in the report.

Stanley J. Czerwinski
Director, Strategic Issues

Appendix I: Objectives, Scope, and Methodology

To better understand grant management lessons resulting from the American Recovery and Reinvestment Act of 2009 (Recovery Act), we focused on two key issues involving grant implementation during the Recovery Act: accountability and transparency. Specifically, this report identifies and provides examples of good practices employed and the challenges faced by select federal, state, and local agencies implementing grant programs funded by the Recovery Act, in the areas of accountability and transparency.

To obtain a broad view of lessons learned during the implementation of grants funded by the Recovery Act, we conducted a detailed literature review of relevant reports describing lessons learned from implementing grants funded by the Recovery Act from GAO; federal and state inspectors general; federal agencies; state and local governments; accountability boards; state and local government advocacy organizations; think tanks; and academia.[1] We developed selection criteria to identify relevant federal agencies and state and local governments to obtain their views related to the implementation of grant programs funded by the Recovery Act. We then selected four federal agencies, three states, and two localities based on the extent to which they had information related to our focus areas of accountability and transparency; information from our colleagues, subject matter experts, and academics; and citations in the literature. To capture a diverse mix of Recovery Act grants and identify potential good practices and challenges, we selected a variety of grants—some that had their funding structures already well established, others that had their funding greatly increased as a result of the Recovery Act, as well as new programs.[2] Although Medicaid was the largest grant program funded by the Recovery Act, we deemed it out of scope for the purposes of this review since it is primarily an entitlement and subject to specific rules that are not typical of program grants. Further, Medicare and unemployment insurance were not included in the recipient reports we examined.

To obtain illustrative examples of the good practices employed and the challenges faced during the implementation of grants funded by the Recovery Act related to accountability and transparency, we conducted interviews with a wide range of officials and experts. We interviewed cognizant officials and obtained supporting documentation from government-wide oversight entities at the federal level including the Recovery Implementation Office, Office of Management and Budget, and the Recovery Accountability and Transparency Board. In addition, we interviewed and obtained supporting documentation from select federal agency officials from the Departments of Education; Energy; Housing and Urban Development; and Transportation; and their respective inspectors general. At the state level, we interviewed and obtained supporting documentation from agency and audit officials from the states of California, Georgia, and Massachusetts. To get a broader state perspective, we also interviewed officials from the state Recovery Act coordinators' network, which included key state officials involved in implementing the Recovery Act from several states. 3 At the local level, we interviewed officials from Denver, Colorado and New York, New York.

We also interviewed officials from leading state and local advocacy organizations that were involved in Recovery Act implementation such as the National Association of State Auditors and Comptrollers, the National Association of State Budget Officers, and the National Association of Counties. We obtained additional information on lessons learned related to the Recovery Act from officials representing the Government Accountability and Transparency Board, Sunlight Foundation, Council of Government Relations, National Council of Non-profits, Center for Effective Government, the Federal Demonstration Project, and National Association of State Chief Information Officers. In addition, we conducted seven focus groups representing a range of federal fund recipients.[4] Focus groups included: (1) state comptrollers; (2) state education and transportation officials; and (3) local government officials from both large and small municipalities. Each focus group had between four and eight participants who were recruited from randomized member lists provided by the recipient associations we interviewed.

Lastly, we reviewed and synthesized information provided in previously issued reports related to the Recovery Act that included the following sources: our previous work; inspectors general from the Departments of Education, Energy, Housing and Urban Development, and Transportation; the Recovery Accountability and Transparency Board; the White House; and various non-governmental sources including the IBM Center for The Business of Government. In addition, we reviewed and applied criteria established by HowTo.gov, a source of guidance and leading practices for government websites, to Recovery.gov and state and local Recovery websites. The scope of our work did not include independent evaluation or verification of the effectiveness of the examples we identified. We also did not attempt to assess the prevalence of the practices or challenges we cite either within or across levels of government. Therefore, entities other than those cited for a particular practice may or may not have employed the same or similar practice, and it is not possible to generalize how prevalent the practices and challenges may be across all Recovery Act grants.

We conducted this performance audit from December 2012 through January 2014, in accordance with generally accepted government auditing standards. Those standards require that we plan and perform the audit to obtain sufficient, appropriate evidence to provide a reasonable basis for our findings and conclusions based on our audit objectives. We believe that the evidence obtained provides a reasonable basis for our findings and conclusions based on our audit objectives.

End Notes

[1] Pub. L. No. 111-5, 123 Stat. 115.

[2] The Recovery Act established multiple mechanisms to provide accountability including those aimed at preventing fraud, waste, and abuse. According to the Office of Management and Budget's (OMB) initial Recovery Act implementation guidance, meeting the Recovery Act's accountability objectives included ensuring that funds were awarded and distributed in a prompt manner; benefits of these funds were reported in a timely manner; and projects funded avoided unnecessary delays and cost overruns. OMB further specified that a critical accountability objective is ensuring funds are used for authorized purposes and instances of fraud, waste, and abuse are mitigated. See OMB, *Initial Implementing Guidance for the American Recovery and Reinvestment Act of 2009*, OMB Memorandum M-09-10 (2009).

[3] In 2009, the President and OMB issued memos stating that "transparency promotes accountability and provides information for citizens about what the Government is doing." Further, the Federal Funding Accountability and Transparency Act of 2006, as amended, requires information disclosure concerning entities receiving federal financial assistance through federal awards such as federal contracts, sub-contracts, grants, and sub-grants. 31 U.S.C. § 6101 note. Office of Management and Budget, *Open Government Directive*, OMB Memorandum M-10-06 (2009); and *Open Government Directive–Federal Spending Transparency and Subaward and Compensation Data Reporting* (2010).

[4] GAO, *Federal Data Transparency: Opportunities Remain to Incorporate Lessons Learned as Availability of Spending Data Increases,* GAO-13-758 (Washington, D.C.: Sept. 12, 2013).

[5] For additional information on GAO's broad body of work related to the Recovery Act, see http://www.gao.gov/recovery/. External reports we reviewed include studies by the White House, Recovery Accountability and Transparency Board, federal Inspectors General, IBM Center for the Business of Government, and George Mason University. See appendix I for additional information on studies reviewed.

[6] The Recovery Implementation Office, with a staff of not more than eight full-time equivalents, was created by Vice President Biden to oversee the high-level management dimensions of the Recovery Act. The Recovery Accountability and Transparency Board was created by the Recovery Act to carry out a wide range of accountability and transparency functions. See table 1 for more specifics.

[7] Recovery Act, § 3(a), 123 Stat. at 116.

[8] The authority of the Recovery Board was expanded by the Consolidated Appropriations Act, 2011, under which the Recovery Accountability and Transparency Board was appropriated $28.35 million, to carry out title XV of the Recovery Act and to "develop and test information technology resources and oversight mechanisms to enhance transparency of and detect and remediate waste, fraud, and abuse in federal spending." Pub. L. No. 112-74, 125 Stat. 786, 920 (2011).

[9] Disaster Relief Appropriations Act, 2013, Pub. L. No. 113-2, § 904(d), 127 Stat. 4, 18.

[10] Congressional Budget Office, *Estimated Impact of the American Recovery and Reinvestment Act on Employment and Economic Output from October 2012 Through December 2012*, (Washington, D.C.: Feb. 21, 2013). In January 2010, CBO estimated that the cost of the Recovery Act would be larger than originally estimated. Among the factors contributing to the higher estimates were higher than anticipated use of entitlement programs such as unemployment insurance and nutritional assistance, as well as higher than anticipated use of the Build America Bonds program.

[11] Medicaid is a joint federal-state program that finances health care for certain categories of low-income individuals, including children, families, persons with disabilities, and persons who are elderly.

[12] An "obligation" is the definite commitment that creates a legal liability of the government for the payment of goods and services ordered or received, or a legal duty on the part of the United States that could mature into a legal liability by virtue of actions on the part of the other party beyond the control of the United States. An "outlay" is the issuance of checks, disbursement of cash, or electronic transfer of funds made to liquidate a federal obligation. See GAO, *A Glossary of Terms Used in the Federal Budget Process*, GAO-05-734SP, (Washington, D.C.: Sept. 2005). Spending by the federal government (i.e., funds obligated and outlayed) can represent just the first steps of using the funds. For instance, the Department of Education makes grants to state educational agencies. After the federal government has outlayed the funds to the state educational agencies, they may, in turn, make grants to local educational agencies, which would then, in turn, spend the money on salaries, school facilities, or other items.

[13] Some programs administered by these agencies followed a different procedure. For example, some of the Recovery Act funds provided to the Department of Transportation were distributed to states and localities through the statutory formulas and rules governing existing programs. The states and localities retained responsibility for selecting projects, which were required to meet additional requirements specified in the Act.

[14] Under the Recovery Act, the Department of Education's SFSF Grant authorized three programs—SFSF State Grants, State Incentive Grants, and an Innovation Fund. Of the $53.6 billion appropriated for SFSF, the Department used $48.6 billion for the State Grants, $4.35 million for Race to the Top Grants (authorized under the State Incentive Grants), and $650,000 for the Investing in Innovation program (authorized under the Innovation Fund). Recovery Act, div. A, §§ 14001–14012, 123 Stat. at 279–286.

[15] Although the law gave responsibility to agencies to make recipient reports available, recipients actually submitted information to a single website operated by the Recovery Board. Data were then provided to agencies for review and recipients were requested to make any needed corrections. The Recovery Board then made the data available on its website, Recovery.gov.

[16] The Recovery Accountability and Transparency Board is comprised of a chairperson appointed by the President and inspectors general from the Departments of Agriculture, Commerce, Education, Energy, Health and Human Services, Homeland Security, Justice,

Transportation, and Treasury, and any other inspector general designated by the President from any agency that expends or obligates Recovery Act funds.

[17] GAO, *Managing for Results: Key Considerations for Implementing Interagency Collaborative Mechanisms*, GAO-12-1022 (Washington, D.C.: Sept. 27, 2012); *Streamlining Government: Key Practices from Select Efficiency Initiatives Should be Shared Government wide*, GAO-11-908 (Washington, D.C.: Sept. 30, 2011); *Gulf Coast Rebuilding: Preliminary Observations on Progress to Date and Challenges for the Future*, GAO-07-574T (Washington, D.C.: Apr. 12, 2007); and *Catastrophic Disasters: Enhanced Leadership, Capabilities, and Accountability Controls Will Improve the Effectiveness of the Nation's Preparedness, Response, and Recovery System*, GAO-06-618 (Washington, D.C.: Sept. 6, 2006).

[18] OMB, *Initial Implementing Guidance for the American Recovery and Reinvestment Act of 2009*, OMB Memorandum M-09-10 (2009).

[19] Mass. Gen. Laws ch. 7, § 4A(e).

[20] For a detailed discussion of this and related issues see, Posner, Paul L., *et. al., Implementation of the Recovery Act: Networks Under Stress,* George Mason University, Centers on the Public Service, (February 2013).

[21] For more information on the concept of an "outcome broker", please see Frank DiGiammarino, *Can Government Work Like Open Table? Innovation in the Collaborative Era* (2012), accessed January 22, 2014, http://www.scribd.com/doc/115361546/Can-Government-Work-Like-OpenTable.

[22] OMB, *Updated Guidance on the American Recovery and Reinvestment Act – Data Quality, Non-Reporting Recipients, and Reporting of Job Estimates*, OMB Memorandum10-08 (2009).

[23] An example of an incident command system can be found within the Department of Homeland Security's (DHS) National Incident Management System, which is intended to provide a consistent framework for incident management at all jurisdictional levels regardless of cause, size, or complexity of the situation. It also defines the roles and responsibilities of federal, state, and local governments during an emergency event. DHS's system has an incident command system component designed to coordinate the communications, personnel, and procedures of different agencies and levels of government within a common organizational structure during an emergency.

[24] Pub. L. No. 111-352, 124 Stat. 3866. GPRAMA updated the Government Performance and Results Act of 1993 (GPRA). Pub. L. No. 103-62, 107 Stat. 285.

[25] GAO, *Managing for Results: Data-Driven Performance Reviews Show Promise But Agencies Should Explore How to Involve Other Relevant Agencies*, GAO-13-228 (Washington, D.C.: Feb. 27, 2103).

[26] Digital Accountability and Transparency Act of 2013, H.R. 2061, 113th Cong. (2013); Digital Accountability and Transparency Act of 2013, S. 994, 113th Cong. (2013).

[27] *Special Report on The American Recovery and Reinvestment Act at the Department of Energy* (OAS-RA-09-01, March 2009).

[28] GAO, *Highway Infrastructure: Federal-State Partnership Produces Benefits and Poses Oversight Risks*, GAO-12-474 (Washington, D.C.: Apr. 26, 2012).

[29] GAO, *Recovery Act: As Initial Implementation Unfolds in States and Localities, Continued Attention to Accountability Issues is Essential*, GAO-09-580 (Washington, D.C.: Apr. 23, 2009).

[30] GAO, *Recovery Act: States' and Localities' Use of Funds and Actions Needed to Address Implementation Challenges and Bolster Accountability*, GAO-10-604 (Washington, D.C.:

May 26, 2010); and *Recovery Act: One Year Later, States' and Localities' Use of Funds and Opportunities to Strengthen Accountability*, GAO-10-437 (Washington, D.C.: Mar. 3, 2010).

[31] GAO-10-604.

[32] GAO, *Highlights of a Forum: Data Analytics for Oversight and Law Enforcement*, GAO-13-680SP (Washington, D.C.: July 2013).

[33] GAO, *Recovery Act: Funding Used for Transportation Infrastructure Projects, but Some Requirements Proved Challenging*, GAO-11-600 (Washington, D.C.: June 29, 2011) and *Recovery Act: Planned Efforts and Challenges in Evaluating Compliance with Maintenance of Effort and Similar Provisions*, GAO-10-247 (Washington, D.C.: Nov. 30, 2009).

[34] Recovery Act, div. A, § 1201(a), 123 Stat. at 212.

[35] Although the Energy Efficiency Conservation Block Grant was authorized in 2007 by the Energy Independence and Security Act of 2007, it was not funded (and the monies could not be spent) until the Recovery Act was enacted in 2009 and therefore is considered a new program.

[36] See http://www.howto.gov/about-us, accessed December 12, 2013.

[37] GAO, *Managing for Results: Leading Practices Should Guide the Continued Development of Performance.gov*, GAO-13-517 (Washington, D.C.: June 6, 2013).

[38] See http://www.mass.gov/recovery/, accessed December 12, 2013.

[39] *Facebook* is a social networking website that allows registered users to create profiles, upload photos and video, and send messages. *Twitter* is a social networking microblogging service that allows members to broadcast short posts called tweets. Twitter members can broadcast tweets and follow other users' tweets on multiple platforms and devices. *YouTube* is a video-sharing website that allows members to store and share video content. *Flickr* is an image hosting and video hosting website that allows users to share and embed photographs.

[40] A feed is a regularly updated summary of new content that also links to the content. The RSS feed allows Recovery.gov to publish frequently updated information by syndicating content automatically.

[41] *Tumblr* is a microblogging platform and social networking website which allows users to post multimedia and other content to a short-form blog.

[42] See http://nycarra.tumblr.com/, accessed December 12, 2013.

[43] An API specifies how some software components should interact with each other. APIs make it easier for software to interact with an outside program like a database or computer service such as a display control.

[44] A widget is an application that allows a website to perform a function, ranging from displaying a simple clock to pulling data from multiple sources for display. Recovery.gov provides widgets that let users display state-level recipient data or search the Recovery.gov databases from their own websites.

[45] When measuring the implementation of Recovery Act, both the amount and speed of grant funding can be thought of as *output measures*. These measures typically describe an activity or effort including a description of the characteristics (e.g., amount or timeliness) established as standards for the activity (in this case grant funding). In contrast, *outcome measures* provide an assessment of results compared to the intended purpose to be achieved.

[46] These reports were submitted to FederalReporting.gov, the central governmentwide data collection system for federal agencies and recipients of federal awards using Recovery Act funds.

[47] 31 U.S.C. § 6101 note.

[48] GAO, *Recovery Act: As Initial Implementation Unfolds in States and Localities, Continued Attention to Accountability Issues is Essential*, GAO-09-580 (Washington, D.C.: Apr. 23, 2009).

[49] GAO, *Federal Data Transparency: Opportunities Remain to Incorporate Recovery Act Lessons Learned,* GAO-13-871T (Washington, D.C.: Sept. 18, 2013); *Federal Data Transparency: Opportunities Remain to Incorporate Lessons Learned as Availability of Spending Data Increases*, GAO-13-758 (Washington, D.C.: Sept. 12, 2013); and GAO-13-680SP.

[50] After the first few quarters of Recovery Act reporting, the system stabilized so recipients generally only needed to update a few data fields each cycle.

[51] OMB staff agreed that the Government Accountability and Transparency Board's early plan provides an initial strategy and added that multiple initiatives are under way. One of these initiatives is the administration's fiscal year 2014 budget proposal that would operationalize comprehensive transparency through the transfer of USAspending.gov from the General Services Administration to the Department of the Treasury.

[52] This report was issued by the Department of Interior's OIG on behalf of the Recovery Board and included input from sixteen agencies and their OIGs. For more, see U. S. Department of Interior, Office of the Inspector General, *Lessons Learned from the Recovery Act: An Agency and OIG Retrospective*, Report No. RO-SP-MOI-0008-2012 (Washington, D.C.: May 2013).

[53] See GAO-12-913T.

[54] GAO-13-871T and GAO-13-758.

[55] Recovery Act, div. A, § 1512(c)(3)(D), 123 Stat. at 288.

[56] These reporting requirements applied only to nonfederal recipients of funding, including all entities receiving Recovery Act funds directly from the federal government such as state and local governments, private companies, educational institutions, nonprofits, and other private organizations.

[57] Office of Management and Budget, *Implementing Guidance for the Reports on Use of Funds Pursuant to the American Recovery and Reinvestment Act of 2009*, OMB Memorandum M-09-21 (2009).

[58] GAO, *Recovery Act: Recipient Reported Jobs Data Provide Some Insight into Use of Recovery Act Funding, but Data Quality and Reporting Issues Need Attention*, GAO-10-223 (Washington, D.C.: Nov. 19, 2009).

[59] According to a senior Recovery Board official, in an effort to accommodate weekends and holidays, the Recovery Board regularly allowed recipients 14 days to submit their data to FederalReporting.gov.

[60] See OMB Memorandum M-09-10 (2009). This information was to be provided by all agencies receiving Recovery Act funds, covering each grant program using these funds, in the agencies' "Recovery Program Plans" submitted to OMB. Initially due on May 1, 2009, the plans were to be updated by the agencies as needed and were to be published on Recovery.gov as well as agency websites. These plans included information on each Recovery Act program's objectives, activities, delivery schedule, accountability plan, monitoring plan, and program performance measures.

[61] GAO, *Recovery Act: States' and Localities' Use of Funds and Actions Needed to Address Implementation Challenges and Bolster Accountability*, GAO-10-604 (Washington, D.C.: May 26, 2010).

[62] Digital Accountability and Transparency Act of 2013, H.R. 2061, 113th Cong. (2013); Digital Accountability and Transparency Act of 2013, S. 994, 113th Cong. (2013).

End Notes for Appendix I

[1] External reports reviewed include Khademian, Anne and Sang Choi, *Virginia's Implementation of the American Recovery and Reinvestment Act: Forging a New Intergovernmental Partnership,* IBM Center for the Business of Government (2011); DeSeve, G. Edward, *Managing Recovery: An Insider's View,* IBM Center for the Business of Government (2011); Posner, Paul L., et. al., *Implementation of the Recovery Act: Networks Under Stress,* George Mason University, Centers on the Public Service, (February 2013); U.S. Department of the Interior, Office of Inspector General, *Lessons Learned from the Recovery Act: An Agency and OIG Retrospective,* RO-SP-MOI-0008- 2012 (Washington, D.C.: May 2013); White House, *A New Way of Doing Business: How the Recovery Act is Leading the Way to 21st Century Government,* (February 2012); Rojas, Francisca M., *Recovery Act Transparency: Learning from States' Experience,* IBM Center for the Business of Government (2012); Callahan, Richard, Sandra O. Archibald, Kay A. Sterner, and H. Brinton Milward, *Key Actions That Contribute to Successful Program Implementation: Lessons from the Recovery Act,* IBM Center for the Business of Government (2012); U.S. Department of Energy, Office of Inspector General ,Office of Audits and Inspections, *Lessons Learned/Best Practices during the Department of Energy's Implementation of the American Recovery and Reinvestment Act of 2009,* OASRA-12-03 (Washington, D.C.: January 2012); and, U.S. Department of Housing and Urban Development, Office of Inspector General, *American Recovery and Reinvestment Act Lessons Learned Initiative,* Memorandum No.: 2013-IE-0801, (October 18, 2012).

[2] The specific grants we focused on were: DOE, Energy Efficiency and Conservation Block Grant and the Weatherization Assistance Program; at DOT, Transportation Investment Generating Economic Recovery (TIGER) grants and the Federal Aid Highway Program; at HUD, Community Development Block Grants and the Tax Credit Assistance Program; at Education, Race to the Top grants, and the State Fiscal Stabilization Fund.

[3] The states represented in the state Recovery Act coordinators' network meeting were Arizona, Arkansas, Delaware, Florida, Maryland, Massachusetts, Michigan, Minnesota, Missouri, Nebraska, Nevada, Oregon, Rhode Island, Tennessee, Texas, Utah, and Wisconsin.

[4] Results from nongeneralizable samples cannot be used to make inferences about a population.

INDEX

D

E

F

G

H

I

J

L

T

U

V

W